W9-BMT-164

Barb Parlette
438-7997

IT TAKES TWO JUDGES TO TRY A COW

AND OTHER STRANGE LEGAL TWISTS

**ERIC CHODAK
AND
BARRY SELTZER**

❖

Canadian Cataloguing in Publication Data

Chodak, Eric, 1949-1991
  It takes two judges to try a cow & other strange
legal twists

Includes index.
ISBN 1-895856-00-0

1. Law-Humor.   I. Seltzer, Barry 1951-
II. Title.

K183.C46 1992   340'.0207   C92-095767-6

Published by
Prism Publishing Inc.
2642 Eglinton Avenue East, Suite 101
Scarborough, Ontario M1K 2S3

Illustrations by David Shaw
Designed by David Shaw and Robert MacPherson
Manufactured by York Bookbinders Inc.
Printed and bound in Canada.

Contents

Foreword / 6

Reasonable People

The Heart That Bounced / 9
The Groom Who Did Backflips /11
The One-Eyed Movie Buff / 15
Lawyer Dates Condom Machine /16
The Lady in the Lavatory / 18
Man Leaps While Hospital Sleeps /21

They Should Have Stayed in Bed!

Driven Over, Then Shot in the Leg / 25
The Epileptic Ambulance Driver / 27
Surgery by Explosion / 30
She *Really* Should Have Stayed in Bed / 32

Anomalies

The Pot of Gold / 35
The Case of the Political Landlady / 38
The Husband and the Vase / 40

Marriage

One of Life's Greatest Lies / 45
In the Clearing Lies a Boxer / 47
With or Without a Condom — There's the Rub! / 51
Love Me, Love My Wife, Wife /52
Sex, Yes — But Not With My Husband / 54
Patience Is a Virtue — But Seventeen Years? / 56
Whose Dress Is It, Anyway? / 57
Artificial Insemination — Adultery or Not? / 59
Surprise! I Just Got Sterilized! / 61

All About Love

He Says "I Do ": He Says "Me Too." / 65
I'll Marry You, I Promise / 67
Will You Love Me When I'm Old? / 69

Married Woman Sues Due to Sexual Solicitation / 70
Are You a Boy or Are You a Girl? / 72
In the Arms of Another Man / 75
Poison Him, Then Sue Him / 76

❖ **Poor Social Skills**

Fig Your Love / 79
If I Lose, I'll Spit in Your Face / 81
The Human Shield / 83
The Serrated Guest / 87
I Am a Blabber Mouth / 89

❖ **Lawyers and Judges**

It Takes Two Justices to Try a Cow / 93
The Evidence That Wouldn't Stand Up / 94
The Case of the Kissing Judge / 96
The Legal Merry-Go-Round / 98
Pants That Kill / 100
The Defence Rests / 101

❖ **House Calls Would Be Safer**
The Surgeon Juggler /105
The Student Lab Animal / 108
Unorthodox Therapy / 113
That's Gratitude for You / 115

❖ **Landowners**
The Landlord Was Jealous / 121
Landlord Raises the Roof / 123
You Pays Your Taxes and Takes Your Chances / 125
The Moths of Hope / 127
Lawyer Makes the Earth Move / 129
Cemetery Evicts Its Tenants / 131

❖ **Travel**
Unchained Melody / 135
Passengers Walk the Plank / 137
Look Before You Leap / 141
Dining and Whining /144
It's Three Stooges Time /147

❖ **Miscellany**
Hear No Evil / 151
Two to Love / 152
The Rat Race / 155
Police Detain Porky Pigs / 159
She Got the Chair – In the Air / 160
The Besmeared Banker / 163

❖ **Finalé**
A Bull in a China Shop — *Really* / 165

Acknowledgements / 167

List of Abbreviations / 169

Source Notes / 171

Foreword

About two years ago, my brother Eric, a lawyer, was told that he had lung cancer. We were all very shaken and upset by this news.

Eric had been ill more than half his life. At age eighteen he was diagnosed with schleroderma, an incurable disease characterized by pain, fatigue, and the gradual deformity of the body. Since that time, he had frequently been hospitalized. Nonetheless, Eric had completed his education and then built and maintained a successful law practice, earning the respect of judges, fellow lawyers, and clients. In spite of his precarious health, he had fervently pursued his many interests, including film, theatre, travel, and writing. He possessed a sharp wit and an incredible mind. Eric was a devoted son, brother, uncle, and friend, and we were devastated to realize that we would lose him.

Around the time of Eric's diagnosis, my husband Barry, also a lawyer, had decided that he would write a book comprising some of the more bizarre legal cases and judgments he had come across in his reading. As he watched Eric's health begin to deteriorate during the summer of 1991, Barry realized that his brother-in-law's spirit and perseverance were also beginning to wane. Perhaps, thought Barry, a project, such as a book, would inspire Eric to continue his fight.

Eric agreed to co-write the book with Barry. Many long hours were spent at Eric's dining-room table assembling cases and writing. For a while Eric seemed renewed and enthused. The cancer, however, continued to ravage his lungs, and soon he was incapacitated, requiring oxygen and nursing care.

On November 6,1991, Eric passed away quietly and with dignity in his home with myself, Barry and our cousin Mark by his side.

Knowing Eric as I did, I recognized that his decision to co-author the book was an act of friendship and selflessness. Eric recognized that Barry was having difficulty accepting the inevitable result of this illness. At the same time, Barry had hoped that the book would give Eric something that would keep him fighting — a focus that could go beyond death.

This is why I say that this book is about friendship, dedication, perseverance, and love. It is about two brothers-in-law, who, each in his own way, was trying to sustain and shoulder the other. It is a memorial to my brother and a symbol of my husband's love and kindness.

It is also a very funny book, funnier because everything in it is true. Enjoy it — I know that Eric and Barry enjoyed writing it.

Francine Seltzer , October 1992

REASONABLE PEOPLE

The Heart That Bounced

Louise Campeau, a beautiful woman of thirty-five, unfortunately had severe cardiac problems necessitating a heart transplant. Of course, such procedures take time, and it was two years before an exact match was found for Louise's blood type, et cetera. The donor was a twenty-four-year-old, very athletic, energetic male who had died in a motorcycle accident.

Louise was admitted to hospital and underwent the lengthy and difficult operation. It went well, Louise came out of the anaesthetic nicely, and for two days all seemed perfect. Then Louise began thrashing about in her hospital bed. Dr. Seymour Mankewitz, one of the surgeons who had performed the operation, expressed his concern, but Louise seemed to recover from this setback and progressed "as well as can be expected."

She was finally released from hospital, but as time went on, she noticed strange urges. For instance, she felt compelled to do cartwheels and backflips in social situations where these were unacceptable. She also suffered seizures.

When she felt well enough, Louise and some friends went to a fancy restaurant for a very expensive meal to celebrate the success of the transplant. The entrée was barely served when Louise felt the need to do somersaults and headstands around the dining-room. She also noticed that when she and her boyfriend tried to get away for an amorous weekend, the result was embarrassing and unfulfilling. The only activity Louise felt like engaging in on the bed was jumping up and down on it as if it were a trampoline.

What ultimately brought Louise to launch her lawsuit against the hospital, Dr. Seymour Mankewitz, and the other surgeons involved, was her behaviour at her uncle's funeral. During the eulogy, she felt an absolutely unstoppable urge to do cartwheels down the aisle of the funeral home. She was, she stated, extremely embarrassed and frightened by this turn of events.

Louise had found out that the donor of her heart had been an acrobat in a circus, and this, she felt, was the cause of her unseemly behaviour. Alleging that the doctor's negligence had destroyed her life, Louise sued her surgeons for $10 million. Though Dr. Seymour Mankewitz refused to make any comments in relation to the lawsuit, his lawyer, Jon R. Moss, announced that "the suit was both preposterous and utterly absurd."

Does Louise's heart still leap at the sound of a calliope? Is she still performing cartwheels in funeral homes? More to our point — did she win her case? Presumably it's still under deliberation, but logic tells us that the "causal" connection between Louise's surgery and her behaviour would be more than a little difficult to prove here.

Let's move on to further calisthenics . . .

The Groom Who Did Backflips

Y ou never know a person until you live with him or her for a while and sometimes not even then. A lady we shall know only as Miss Witaker discovered that simple truth in a way few people have.

Miss Witaker found a certain Mr. McNielly, recently discharged from military service, sufficiently appealing that she accepted his marriage proposal. We are given no intimations of McNielly's behaviour during his courtship with Miss Witaker, but the marriage was a bizarre disaster from the start. McNielly giggled all through the ceremony. When asked the usual questions by the minister he erupted in hysterical laughter. Miss Witaker, no doubt trying to remain hopeful, and the wedding guests, no doubt trying to be charitable, apparently attributed this conduct to that of a nervous groom.

At the reception, things only got worse. McNielly entered the reception hall by way of handsprings and backflips. This, you would think, *had* to cause concern. But it seems that, being hopeful and charitable folk, the bride and her guests chalked the acrobatics up to an excess of nuptial exuberance. Things continued to go markedly downhill. McNielly responded to a beautiful toast to the bride by making an obscene toast and telling a series of filthy stories. Dinner was served as planned, and the by now slightly alarmed guests valiantly endeavoured to keep things festive.

The reception came to its inevitable conclusion, and the bride and groom headed for home — McNielly's home — where Miss Witaker naturally expected McNielly to fulfill his manly obligations. Instead, he told his bride of a few hours to go home and not bother him. Miss Witaker now began to wonder seriously if her spouse was in touch with reality. She asked herself for the first time — but certainly not the last — whether McNielly even realized he was married.

Amazingly, poor Miss Witaker found herself still very much in love with her strange husband. Against all reason, she stayed with him. Eventually, during a train ride from their British Columbia home to New Brunswick, they consummated the marriage.

Alas, McNielly's mind continued to deteriorate. At one point he barricaded himself in the bedroom for two weeks and demanded

milk bottles in which to relieve himself. Later, after they bought a new house, he took to relieving himself on the floor. He once threw a pot of hot potatoes at his hapless wife, and on another occasion pushed her out of a truck that happened to be in motion. He attacked his mother-in-law with a carving knife. One day he claimed to have been attacked by wolves, and once he accused his wife of being the head of the narcotics trade in Canada.

The couple bought a motor hotel, and, for a short time, McNielly managed to run it reasonably well. But he started to favour renting the rooms to the local prostitute population, and one morning, at three o'clock, he suddenly ordered every guest to leave. He blamed his "war nerves," although the only war he ever served in was that between sanity and psychosis perpetually raging in his own fevered brain. He continued to suffer from obsessions and illusions and became progressively more violent.

Finally, *finally*, McNielly was referred to a psychiatrist. It did not take the doctor long to diagnose McNielly as suffering from incurable paranoid schizophrenia.

What about the court case? After all, isn't this a book about court cases? Well, Miss Witaker went to court seeking not a divorce, as you might have expected, but rather the far less common procedure known as an annulment. The difference between the two is that a divorce terminates an existing marriage, but an annulment is a judicial declaration that the marriage never existed at all. An annulment can be granted only under very limited circumstances, one of which is mental illness so severe that the person suffering from it was unable to grasp that he or she was entering into the legal contract known as marriage.

The presiding judge came to the conclusion that McNielly was in fact too far gone at the time of the wedding to realize he was getting married, and granted Miss Witaker her decree of annulment.

The One-Eyed Movie Buff

At the age of fifty-seven, Charlie Moore, a hunter and a movie buff, lost the sight of an eye in a hunting accident. (He couldn't very well have lost it in a movie accident, now could he?)

As soon as he had recovered sufficiently he continued his usual Saturday-night outings to the local cinema, the same as he'd done every Saturday night for years. But something had changed. Charlie found that he couldn't see what he referred to as "the whole picture" without constantly turning his head back and forth. He decided that, because of his accident, he was no longer getting his money's worth compared to the other patrons. He cornered the manager and demanded a 50 per cent refund on the price of the twenty-eight films he'd seen since his unfortunate mishap. The manager (after he stopped laughing, presumably) pointed out that although Charlie may have had only one eye, he still possessed two bottom cheeks which collectively took up one seat, not half a seat.

Charlie and the manager had been buddies for years, but at one point their argument got so heated that the two of them nearly came to blows, and the next morning Charlie filed a lawsuit seeking a judicial declaration that would require the theatre to let him in for half price.

At the time of writing, this case is in its initial phases, so we can't tell you if Charlie is enjoying his Saturday-night outings once again. One thing's for sure though: it's the end of a beautiful friendship.

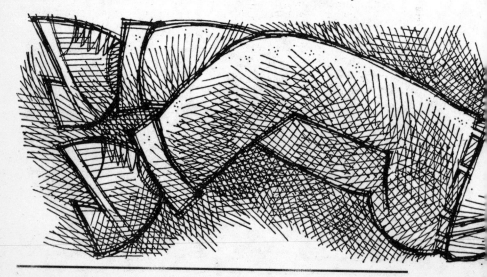

Lawyer Dates Condom Machine

Although the following situation has not yet turned into full-blown litigation, that could happen at any second, and so we felt compelled to tell you about lawyer Alan Glaze of Australia (where they call them solicitors) and his friend and fellow lawyer, Robert Gold.

Alan is twenty-four years young, an age for partying and wild-oat sowing, and having spent the last eight years studying and working in the gruelling world of law, he's really looking forward to a day off. He and his buddy Robert are going to go to a "swinging Brisbane nightclub." They've arranged to meet two young ladies and have high expectations for the evening.

At the nightclub, Robert introduces Alan to his date and Alan is immediately smitten. This, he decides, is going to be one of those nights for the memory book. Alan gazed into her eyes; she gazed back, it was lust at first sight. Valentines, fire crackers, and oh God, Alan remembered all those ethics lectures in law school. The evening wore its magical way on, and things, to Alan's mind anyway, got better and better. Eventually Alan found it necessary to seek out the condom-vending machine in the men's lavatory (that's what they call the washroom in Australia).

The hour was late and Alan felt a certain urgency. He sidled coolly up to the machine hanging on the tiled wall, deposited the exact change, pulled the lever and . . . nothing.

Motivated by love and raging hormones, he anxiously shot his

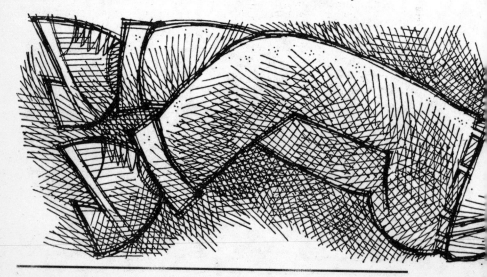

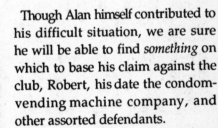

finger gently into the orifice of the machine . . . still nothing. Next he gingerly moved his hand further into the bowels of this mechanical frustration . . . nothing. Would the promise of the evening remain unfulfilled? Further still, and . . . Alan had the great misfortune of getting his hand completely and irretrievably stuck in the condom machine on the wall of the men's toilet.

Valiantly, he sought to free himself in hopes of seeking alternative services. Alas, the harder he struggled, the tighter he stayed caught. He was too embarrassed to scream for help, and eventually he settled in, hoping that someone would come to his rescue in time to avoid ruining the entire evening.

Last call fast came and went. Alan's date, thinking she has been ditched, left the club steaming. Robert, returning to the table with his girl, thought that Alan and his date had left together.

Alan and the condom-vending machine spent the night, and most of the following day, closely linked.

Finally club staff members found him and managed to free him, and, wouldn't you know it, as his hand came free, a shower of condoms fell to the floor.

Though Alan himself contributed to his difficult situation, we are sure he will be able to find *something* on which to base his claim against the club, Robert, his date the condom-vending machine company, and other assorted defendants.

You know, getting into difficult situations in washrooms can happen to just about anyone.

The Lady in the Lavatory

Oh dear, what can the matter be?
Seven old ladies locked in the lavatory.
They were there from Monday to Saturday,
Nobody knew they were there.

Parody of an old English folksong

Very funny, you say, getting locked in a public washroom. Eileen Sayers, of Bishop's Stortford, in Hertfordshire, England, to whom the dread event really happened in 1956, didn't think it very funny at all.

Eileen and her husband were waiting for a bus to take them to London for a long-planned outing when Eileen felt the call of nature, what the English refer to as the need to "spend a penny." The bus wasn't due for another twenty minutes so that left plenty of time. Eileen put her penny in the slot (the source of the idiom), the stall door swung open, and she entered it. Just as the door slammed shut, Eileen noticed to her horror that the inside handle was broken. There was no apparent way out. There was no attendant. There were no other users of this particular public convenience. Eileen Sayers was a prisoner in a toilet stall.

What to do? First, she wondered if there was any way she could manipulate the lock with her finger. There was not. Too little of the mechanism was left. She banged on the cubicle door. With only ten minutes left until the bus was supposed to arrive, you can be sure that she banged animatedly. No response.

It should be mentioned here that the English public lavatories of the day were designed on a grand scale, particularly the penny-in-the-slot variety. After all, can you expect anyone to pay if they are able to slither in above or below the door? This particular cubicle had doors that were seven feet tall. Yet there was a small gap up there, and the over-the-door route seemed the only possible way out. Dauntless, Eileen gave it a try.

Eileen firmly planted both feet on the seat of the lavatory. In her left hand she grasped the pipe running from the overhead cistern.

For that extra boost she knew she needed on the right, she then placed her right foot on the toilet roll. Valiantly, she boosted herself up enough to peer over the door. Imagine her consternation, having expended all that energy, to discover that the gap between the door and the ceiling was just a tad over two feet. Even if she had found the strength to hoist herself up the rest of the way there was no possibility of her squeezing through.

Not seeing much in the way of alternatives, Eileen decided to get down. For a fateful moment she allowed her weight to rest fully on the toilet roll. Alas, the toilet roll had been waiting all its life for this rare opportunity to be true to its name. It rolled.

Eileen went sprawling and crashed to the ground. Fortunately she was not seriously injured, her dignity being the primary victim, however, she suffered painful bruising and considerable discomfort, not to mention the embarrassment she felt when she was finally rescued, her skirt dishevelled and her husband agitated almost to the point of insensibility.

Eileen felt the need for compensation. After all, is there not an implied warranty on the part of the owner of a public facility that the facility is safe for public use? Was the owner not under a duty to inspect and repair the cubicle; at least to warn potential users of any danger? Did it not constitute negligence for the owner to do otherwise? Eileen sued the owners of the lavatory, the Harlow Urban District Council.

Amazingly, the county court judge who heard the trial held that yes, the county was negligent, but that the negligence placed Eileen in no danger. He held, rather, that her injuries flowed *solely* from Eileen's embarking on what he called a "dangerous manoeuvre," and that it was therefore for Eileen to bear the consequences. He found in favour of the council. In plain English — he threw the case out of court.

Man Leaps While Hospital Sleeps

Not all cases we report are humorous; some are downright sad. Gerald Lepine's is one of those. He had better treatment from his hotel than from the hospital.

Gerald, an Indian who lived at Hay River in the Northwest Territories, had suffered from epilepsy since he was thirteen. The type of epilepsy that plagued him was known as automatism. Most victims of automatism do not move about during seizures, but a minority, which included Gerald, do move from place to place while the seizure renders them oblivious to their movements. Such patients are in no way responsible for their actions, but they represent a considerable danger, both to themselves and to others.

Gerald had always been a co-operative patient, faithfully following his doctor's advice. Eventually, that doctor referred him to Dr. Monckton in Edmonton, a neurologist. While in Edmonton, Gerald stayed at the King Edward Hotel. One evening shortly after midnight, a hotel security guard found Gerald on the roof of the hotel. He was having a seizure. The police were sent for, and realizing his condition, returned Gerald to his room.

The conscientious security guard kept him under observation until 3:00 AM, when he had another seizure. During this attack the hotel security officer placed himself between Lepine and the fire escape. Lepine tried to go out the window, but the guard had him sit on the bed in the room until the police arrived.

After a third attack, Gerald was taken by ambulance to University Hospital and admitted to a room on the fourth floor. During his two-day stay, he suffered twenty-eight epileptic seizures. At times he wandered out of his room for some distance. He was difficult and noisy. His speech was incoherent and rapid, and he was making odd movements.

Finally he wandered away from the hospital dressed only in his robe, pyjamas, socks, and wearing no shoes. He was found by police officers and informed them that "The nuts in the hospital have a bomb." When the police returned him to the hospital, he told them, in the presence of an orderly, to go ahead and shoot him, he had nothing left.

The three police officers, the orderly, and nurses took Gerald to his room. It was an ordinary hospital room: the bed near the window, a chair beside the bed. Gerald walked over to the chair and sat down, asking if he could put on his shoes. "We had no objection," said a police officer. "He seemed quite calm then."

He then asked to use the washroom, which was in the room. Dr. Monckton came in with another nurse, and when Gerald came out of the washroom (with a sort of half-grin on his face, according to witnesses), the doctor asked him how he was feeling. "Just fine," he answered.

As Lepine started walking towards the bed, he suddenly took two steps, leaped up on the chair and dove right out through the window to the ground, four storeys below.

Gerald survived his dramatic plunge but with permanent disabilities. Later he sued Dr. Monckton for, among other things, failing to have him treated in a special ward with unbreakable windows, failing to have him restrained, not keeping him on the ground floor, and failing to provide proper supervision and medication. He sued the hospital for failing to provide proper care, treatment, and protection.

The trial judge dismissed Lepine's action against Dr. Monckton, saying that the doctor was not guilty, but that "at the very most [it was] an error of judgment and that in itself is no cause of action." He added that a man, "especially a man of eminence in his own branch of the profession, can't devote his whole time to any one patient, and it seems to me that there is no evidence of any negligence." However, he found the hospital to be responsible for Lepine's injuries, saying, "with all respect, it would appear obvious to any intelligent high school student that it was dangerous [to leave Lepine] without safeguards."

The hospital did what any good hospital would do . . . it appealed the decision. The Court of Appeal, however, said that not only was the hospital responsible, so was Dr. Monckton. The Supreme Court, when appealed to, provided this insight: "Despite his severe and permanent disabilities, [Lepine] impressed me as being sincerely honest and quietly courageous in his outlook on life, without any tendency to self pity. This is one of those 'hard cases' . . . "

A "hard case" for Gerald, in the opinion of the court, but not for the doctor or the hospital. For the hospital to have put Lepine at ground level or to have restrained him was neither required nor necessary according to the court. It surely could not have anticipated that Gerald would suddenly leap through the window. While he did have twenty-eight seizures, was incoherent, asked the police to shoot him, believed the hospital had a bomb, and made odd movements, he did not actually write a letter telling anyone in the hospital he planned to leap out of the window beside his bed.

Perhaps he should have taken the security guard with him from the King Edward Hotel.

THEY SHOULD HAVE STAYED IN BED!

Driven Over, Then Shot in the Leg

At times, we all search for a way to break up the monotony of our day-to-day existence. Sometimes, when we get what we wish for, we realize that the status quo was really not too bad.

George Robert Baker is not what you might call a lucky fellow. In fact, you would never want to go in on a lottery ticket with him. George, of Mitcham Common in England, early one Saturday decided to break up the boredom of the weekend by going out for a drive with a friend in the friend's car. Shortly into their excursion they ran out of petrol (what the English call gas).

His buddy was offered a lift to the nearest gas station by a passing motorist. Realizing as he crossed the street that not only had he forgotten to fill up, but he had left his wallet at home, he called across the road to George to loan him a few quid.

Patient George obligingly set off across the road, wallet in hand. First he looked to his right (remember this is England. Cars drive on the *other* side) and saw only one other car on the road. He started to move across the road. Woops! Hasn't he forgotten something? Not until he got to the centre of the street did George look to his left. Obviously, he had forgotten all those lessons parents, schools, and crossing guards teach children.

Along comes Arthur Willoughby. It's a Saturday morning, the

weather is clear, and there is really not much traffic, so Arthur is fairly barreling along. He decides to pass the vehicle ahead of him, the one George had spotted on his right . . . you might almost think that Arthur *intended* to ruin George's day.

George was a real optimist, always looking on the bright side of life. As he flew through the air, he couldn't help thinking that things were not too bad — at least he wouldn't have to pay for the petrol now.

George suffered injuries to his leg and ankle which caused him, after his release from hospital, to walk with a limp. But look on the bright side, a limping George had a better case against Arthur.

No longer able to work at his old job, George immediately went to work in a scrap-metal yard. (Cars without engines are easier to dodge when you have a limp.) While he was alone at the yard one day, two armed bandits came in and demanded money. Perhaps George thought they were trying to collect for the petrol his friend had had to put into his car. Perhaps he didn't have any. Whatever, George didn't turn over a penny. The robbers shot in his general direction to frighten him, but they did not know lucky George!

The bullet lodged in George's stiff leg. It was now injured to the point where it had to be amputated.

This was not the highlight of George's week, but Arthur's lawyers were thrilled. They submitted to the court that since the gunshot injury removed the very limb which their client ran over, George's lawsuit should be dismissed. George, in effect, didn't have a leg to stand on.

The judge, however, realized that while dodging cars without engines had been within George's ability, dodging bullets could not be done with a stiff leg. The court highlighted this idea by stating: "He could not run before the second injury; he could not run now."

Had George been considerate enough to have died from the gunshot, Arthur might have been off the hook, but now George will suffer from the car accident for as long as he would have done had his leg never been shot and amputated.

The Epileptic Ambulance Driver

Lauren Lucas was attending to business one day in the order office of Sears, Roebuck and Co. in Juneau, Alaska. As one might expect in an office, there was the usual clerical ammunition of pens, stationery, and pencils lying around. This particular day, a round, medium-length pencil was lying in wait for Lauren. Hastening on his daily round, Lauren stepped on this round pencil, which lay in ambush on the floor. He placed his weight fully onto it, causing it to roll to safety, taking Lauren with it. Several seconds of contortions later, Lauren did a spectacular pratfall onto the floor, causing some serious injury to his back.

Lauren was taken to the local hospital where he languished for eighteen days before it was decided that he should be treated at Veteran's Hospital in Seattle.

Perhaps Mr. Lucas should have had an inkling that problems lay ahead when the City of Juneau ambulance showed up, driven by a man with what he felt was a sort of vacant, maniacal look. Perhaps when he was stuffed into the ambulance to be taken to the airport freight transport he should have politely declined, claiming miraculous recovery or previous engagement. But really, Lauren's back *hurt* and those of you who suffer back pain will understand why he did not decline.

Initially the trip was uneventful, but part-way to the airport, the driver was seized with a grand mal epileptic fit. This interfered with normal safe-driving practices. The ambulance headed off the highway, over an embankment, Mr. Lucas was sent sailing off the ambulance cot, hit the wall, bounced nicely onto the floor, and generally aggravated the Sear's-generated back injury.

Much later, after he had obtained the necessary treatment for his back injury, Lauren sued Sears for the pencil trip and the City of Juneau for the epileptic driver's slip.

As all good defendants should, both Sears and the City of Juneau took the position that neither could be held responsible. It was now impossible, they both said, to tell to what extent either was responsible for the back injury suffered by Lauren Lucas.

The court said that because "the advice to proceed to Seattle or elsewhere for medical attention is rather common in Alaska" the trip to Seattle was a necessity. Therefore, it seemed to the judge, Sears should pay not only for the pencil trip but also for the epileptic driver's fit.

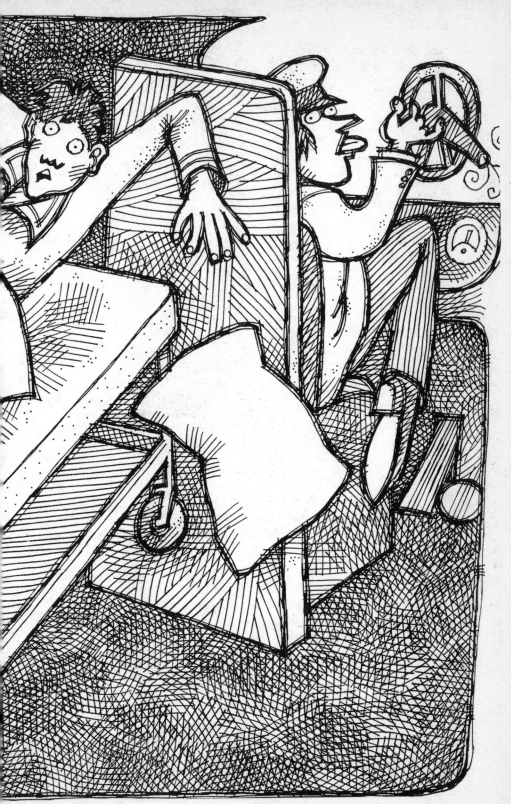

Surgery by Explosion

George Robert Baker was not the only client who should have stayed in bed . . . at home. Young John Crits was in bed in a hospital being prepared for a tonsillectomy. This, we have always been told, is usually a relatively safe operation.

John was first given sodium pentothal to start him on the road to dreamland. He was then connected to an ether can and an oxygen tank. At this point, John must have unconsciously decided that surgeons like colour in their patients, it makes operations so much more interesting. John started to turn blue. Doctor Sylvester and the anaesthetist, noticing the bluish tinge about the patient's lips, decided in a flash of medical agility to correct the condition. The ether can was disconnected — but not turned off — and John was given straight oxygen.

After a moment, Dr. Sylvester, in a sweeping, bending pirouette, disconnected the oxygen bag, intending to reconnect it to the ether can — but no one had turned off the ether.

With a sizzling sound, a flash of blue, and mighty Hi-ho Silver —

sorry, wrong case — a blue flame and a violent explosion shook the operating room. Doctor "Rambo" Sylvester, standing at the foot of the operating table, got the effect, but John was the one who turned colours . . . mostly blue and black.

A spark of static electricity caused by the doctor's motion had set the ether-oxygen mixture on fire. Though it wouldn't have taken a highly trained technician to realize that a dangerous volume of gaseous fumes had built up when the ether was left on, it had slipped by the anaesthetist, the doctor and the nurses.

All operations have inherent risks, but neither John nor his dad Neil would have ever thought that the surgeon intended to blow up tonsils. And while time *is* money, this seems a very drastic form of surgery.

John and his father sued. The anaesthetist, doctor, and hospital did what most competent, soft-spoken medical specialists would do — they handed the file to their liability insurer (a nice name for negligence insurer), who, in turn, handed it to their solicitors. They submitted that it was the usual practice to leave cans of ether that could explode near their patients' heads when they operated. Even the court thought this was going just a little too far and pointed out that the practice of blowing up one's patients was quite unnecessary and should be discouraged. The extra time involved to turn off the gas was insignificant and certainly would not have prevented anyone from making their twelve-o'clock golf game.

She *Really* Should Have Stayed in Bed

Here is another case where the issue before the courts was the apportionment of liability when a second act resulting in injury wouldn't have taken place if the first act — a negligent act — hadn't happened. (We hope that's reasonably clear. After all, a third-year law student would get it.)

Elizabeth Bradford was eating breakfast one morning in a restaurant owned by Gus Kanellos in Kingston, Ontario. The restaurant was laid out in that format familiar to us all: a counter towards the front and tables at the back. As fate would have it, Elizabeth and her husband were seated at the counter. As fate would also have it, someone had forgotten to clean the grill. A menacing-looking flash fire erupted before Elizabeth's horrified eyes.

Fortunately, one of the more level-headed employees activated the fire extinguisher. No one was injured in the fire. So far so good. But the fire extinguisher created a hissing sound, a sound which induced a patron to shout that gas was escaping and that the restaurant was about to join the stratosphere. This observation provoked a stampede in which Elizabeth was thrown from her

stool and trampled. Elizabeth brought a suit against Kanellos, seeking damages for the injuries she sustained during the trampling.

The court's decision could have gone in one of two ways. It could have found that the failure to clean the grill was negligent and that the fire and the stampede were both foreseeable consequences of that negligence. In other words, it could have found in favour of Elizabeth Bradford and awarded her money. (The trial court did just that.) Alternatively, it could have found that while the failure to clean the grill was negligent, and the fire was a foreseeable consequence of that, the stampede was not. Remember that Elizabeth wasn't injured in the fire but in the stampede. If the court favoured this second approach, Elizabeth would lose the case.

Unfortunately for Elizabeth, the Court of Appeal did just that, holding that the stampede was not a foreseeable consequence of Kanellos's negligence in not cleaning his grill. Not only did Elizabeth get nothing, but in accordance with the normal practice in civil cases, she had to pay Kanellos's costs of both the trial and the appeal.

This *had* to be one of the more expensive breakfasts ever served in Kingston. Yes, Elizabeth should have stayed in bed.

ANOMALIES

The Pot of Gold

It's nice to believe in fairy tales. It's nice to dream about winning a lottery. People hunt for treasure on land and at sea, but most of us are aware that all these things are in the realm of fantasy. Some of us, however, operate at different levels of comprehension and motivation. Carrie Nickerson was one of these.

There had long been in her family a rumour to the effect that two long-dead gentlemen of her family had buried a large amount of gold coins on a property owned by John W. Smith. Carrie, a salesperson for the California Perfume Company, visited a fortune teller who told her that it was, indeed, her relatives who had buried the gold and gave her a map supposedly showing its location on the property of Smith.

Aided by three or four of her relatives, Carrie spent several months digging around John Smith's house. Smith extended them a cordial welcome and permitted them to dig almost without limits, and at any time. Perhaps he too had some slight hope that they might find something, and that he would receive a share for his concessions.

Watching as the diggers burrowed around tree roots and house pillars for weeks on end, Smith's daughter "Bud" Baker and her friend H.R. Hayes hatched the plot to provide a treasure for the searchers to find. They got an old copper kettle, filled it with rocks and wet dirt and topped it off with a note written by Hayes directing whoever should find this "pot of gold" to notify all heirs not to open it for three days after finding it. This "treasure" was then buried in the seat of an old chimney as yet untouched by Carrie's group of diggers.

On April 14, Hayes's brother, under the guise of aiding the searchers, dug up the pot and gave the alarm. When the note was discovered, Hayes advised Carrie that he thought its directions should be fulfilled and that the bank was the best place to deposit the "gold" for safe-keeping until the heirs could be notified and the three days were up. The pot was therefore placed in a gunny-sack, tied up, and taken to the bank for deposit.

It didn't take long for the news of the find to spread, and, on hearing about it, the vice-president of the bank went over to the branch to examine the pot so that in the event it did contain gold, proper precautions to guard the bank might be taken. He discovered that the pot contained only dirt. The lid was replaced and it was decided that nothing would be said until Carrie came back several days later.

The secret, however, leaked out, and the matter soon became a joke that, it seemed, everybody but Carrie knew about.

Carrie, meanwhile, had arranged for Judge R.C. Drew to accompany her to the bank for the purpose of seeing that the ceremonies surrounding the opening of the treasure were properly conducted. Half a dozen relatives had been notified and were present at the bank. Bud Baker and H.R. Hayes were also in attendance.

As soon as the sack was brought out the storm began. Carrie, realizing that the string was tied near the top of the sack instead of down low around the pot where she had put it, immediately began to shout that she had been robbed. She flew into a rage and threw the lid of the pot at the cashier. She then turned the force of her wrath on the laughing Hayes. She had to be restrained physically to prevent further violence.

Carrie, who was then forty-five, had, some twenty years before, been an inmate of an insane asylum, a fact which the practical jokers knew well. They had intended what they did to be seen as an April Fool's joke and did not intend Carrie any injury. However, the results were serious indeed. The mental suffering and humiliation were unbearable for Carrie. She died several years later, taking her bitterness and the conviction that she had been robbed to her grave. Before she died she sued the conspirators for mental and physical suffering, humiliation, and injury to her reputation and social standing.

The court established that had she lived, Carrie would have been entitled to substantial damages — sort of "the pot at the end of the rainbow" — but since her legal heirs were the complainants, a judgment of only $500 was granted.

The Case of the Political Landlady

This story could have happened only in America since their two-party system — Democrats *vs.* Republicans — provides the basis for the case.

The expression "politics makes strange bedfellows" is not always true. Sometimes political fellows are asked to vacate their beds. The significance of this was not lost on Jesse Hamrick and Wilson Morrow, two young Indianapolis lawyers who also happened to be staunch Democrats, and who, in consequence, started a most peculiar libel lawsuit in the Superior Court of Indianapolis against their landlady in the late nineteenth century.

Their claim stated that they, being Democrats, intended to vote the Democratic ticket in an upcoming election. Mrs. Sutton, the lady with whom they were boarding, was a staunch Republican, and she had demanded that they vacate their rooms in her home and go elsewhere to have their meals. They claimed that she knew that they could not find another boarding house in the district, and that if she forced them to leave their residence, they would lose their votes.

Mrs. Sutton, claimed Hamrick and Morrow, really had no reason to complain about them, but she, as a Republican, wanted to deprive them, as Democrats, of their right to vote.

Mrs. Sutton openly admitted her Republican leanings, but emphatically denied that politics had anything to do with her actions towards her boarders. She did, however, implore the court to follow good old Will Shakespeare's advice when it comes to lawyers, Republican or Democrat — "The first thing we do," he has a character say in *Henry VI*, "let's kill all the lawyers." Perhaps she didn't want the directive followed to the letter, but in any case, the Superior Court of Indianapolis granted a temporary injunction preventing Mrs. Sutton from getting rid of her two boarders until the trial could be held to hear the case.

Do you think Hamrick and Morrow will now bring action to prevent the boarding-house cook from using anything other than democratic chickens at mealtime?

The Husband and the Vase

Many people have created unusual provisions for their property and estate upon their death, but of these, Henry Crookenden was perhaps at the head of the list. A codicil to his will directed that three days after his death, his body should be given to his friend, Eliza Williams. (He didn't indicate what he'd be up to during the three-day period.) Eliza also received through Henry's will a Wedgewood earthenware vase and

a private letter from Henry directing her what to do with it. The costs and expenses that Eliza might incur in performing Henry's instructions contained in the private letter were to be paid by his executors within three months after his death.

In his letter, Henry instructed Eliza that he should "be burnt when dead or rather under a pile of wood; [he] should like the calcined bones and fragments to be put in the Wedgewood vase or if that was not large enough in any other." The ultimate disposal of the vase and its contents he left entirely to her.

His executors — his widow and one of his sons — had their own

ideas. Henry was buried three days after his death in the unconsecreated part of the Brompton Cemetery with the rites of the Roman Catholic Church. At the funeral, Eliza made some protest as to the disposal of Henry's body, but to no avail.

Several months later, she wrote to the Home Secretary, enclosing copies of both the codicil to the will and the private letter, seeking a licence to remove the body for the purposes of carrying out the wishes of the testator, or, if there were legal impediments or objection, for the purpose of having it buried in consecrated ground. The first part of this request was rejected, but the Under-Secretary of State asked to what burial ground it was proposed to remove the body. Miss Williams responded and was granted a licence to remove the body to another churchyard.

The managers of the Brompton Cemetery informed the solicitors of the widow and sons that the licence had been granted. They immediately wrote to the Secretary of State and the licence was revoked. However, in the meantime, Eliza had had Henry's body disinterred and taken to Milan where it was cremated. She then put the ashes in the Wedgewood vase to be buried in consecrated ground. She, of course, claimed for her expenses in all this, but her claim was rejected by the executors of Henry's estate. This became the subject of a lawsuit.

The court held that there is no property in a dead body. While it may not be the custom to burn bodies, there is no law against doing so. However, the executors are entitled to the possession and are responsible for the burial of a dead body. Eliza Williams had no right of property in Henry's body, nor could she force its delivery by the executors. Furthermore, removal for the purpose of cremation, and, in fact, the cremation itself were illegal acts, and if that alone were the question to be decided it would be impossible for this lady to receive money for the expenses.

Eliza was acting out of the best motives, which she considered a paramount obligation to Henry and his wishes, but this led her to deceive the Home Secretary into granting a licence for a purpose she did not intend to carry out. On the basis of what was done and for any of the reasons reviewed, Eliza's claim for expenses was rejected.

Though Henry wished her to have his mortal remains to deal with in accordance with his private letter, and for her to be reimbursed for doing so, Eliza had no property right in Henry's body and in law was not in a position to carry out Henry's wishes. She did, through deception, fulfill Henry's desire, but she could not be compensated for doing so.

MARRIAGE

One of Life's Greatest Lies

John Papadimitropoulos (we'll call him John) is not the kind of guy you would want your daughter to date (if you have a daughter).

We probably all have our own opinion about what life's greatest lie might be, but certainly John's lie to Dina Karnezi must be one of them. John and Dina were both of Greek origin and lived and worked in Australia. Dina spoke no English; John spoke English well. He apparently also spoke Greek with a silver tongue. Four or five days after John met Dina, who was employed at a factory, he asked her to marry him. He bought her an engagement ring, which she wore happily.

He then asked her to accompany him to the local registry office to be married. Dina's two cousins and an aunt, none of whom spoke English, accompanied the happy couple to the registry office on Queen Street in Melbourne, where they witnessed Dina and John signing a card and a form. These documents were a notice of intention to be married and information to be filled in on a marriage certificate. The pair were not yet married, but John, in Greek, told the party that they were.

John and Dina then went to obtain lodgings. John introduced Dina as his wife, telling the landlady that they had been married that morning.

Over the next four days in that room, John and Dina enjoyed

wedded bliss at least three times. On the fourth day, John told Dina that he had to go the following day to the registry office to collect a document. The next morning, John left the room, never to return. Accompanying him were Dina's savings, which she had had in her purse in the dresser.

This brought a hint of suspicion to Dina's mind that led her to investigate and eventually to uncover John's lie. The unsympathetic landlady turned poor Dina out of the room.

Dina, stating unequivocally that she would never have had intercourse outside of marriage, charged John with rape. The trial judge found that John's offence was a particularly cruel one, and that Dina would never have consented were it not for John's greatest lie. She was consenting to a marital act; what she got was, in the court's opinion, an act of fornication. Her consent was no real consent.

John, now facing a four-year jail term, appealed the conviction to a higher court.

The Court of Appeal reviewed the law, including the history of bigamy and mock marriages, thoroughly. They found that the most heartless bigamist had never been considered a rapist. While it may well have been true that Dina would never have consented to John without marriage, and his conduct was wicked and heartless, none of this was enough to establish that he had committed rape.

Rape is carnal knowledge, physical penetration, of a woman *without her consent*. The consent to physical penetration is the concern; once consent to the identity of the man and the penetration is given, even life's greatest lie cannot make the act rape.

Don't forget John, Dina can still sue you civilly for damages.

In the Clearing Lies a Boxer

Some people collect coins or stamps, others collect autographs of famous personalities. Still others . . . well, Samuel Henry Coley was a rogue who happened to live in New Zealand. One evening in a hotel lounge, he chanced upon a lovely thirty-four-year-old widow, let's call her Sarah. After a very rapid courtship, Sam proposed marriage to Sarah and she accepted, believing everything Sam had told her about his position, his fortune, and his prospects. Three days after they had first met, Sam and Sarah were married. Sarah, however, married someone she knew as Michael Miller. That's the name Sam had used for those three days.

Sam had represented himself to be Michael Miller, a famous Australian boxer. In truth, Sam was not a boxer at all. He was a person of very different fortune from Michael Miller; a person of no fortune at all really.

The audacious fraud was perpetrated successfully not only upon Sarah but upon several of her friends. He would never have had any hope of carrying this fraud through, of saying he was a well-to-do boxer, unless he said what boxer he was. Therefore, he chose the identity of a boxer who was not in New Zealand at the time, and his plan succeeded just long enough.

Two weeks after the wedding, Sarah's money ran out — and so did Sam.

She petitioned for nullity on the ground of fraud. Did Sarah consent to marry the human being to whom she was married by the registrar? Was this a case of real consent induced by fraud or of no consent?

The court concluded that this lady's ambition was to be the wife of the person masquerading as Michael Miller, not to be the wife of that human being who *is* Michael Miller. She was willing to marry this man whom she believed to be able to support her, and the identity of Michael Miller was merely accidental.

Sarah may feel that the state of the law is unfortunate for her, but

fraudulently obtained consent is still consent. "Where marriage is the voluntary act of a person, though brought about by the machinations of other persons, it is good for all purposes and cannot be set aside."

Sarah may wish to first obtain an autographed photograph next time.

With a Condom or Without One.
There's the Rub !

When a court talks about principles being "laid down," normally we understand that the expression is not to be taken in its literal sense. In this case, a certain Mr. Baxter in England asked the court to declare his marriage to Mrs. Baxter a nullity because Mrs. Baxter refused to have sexual relations with him unless he used a condom.

The lower courts decided that because of Mrs. Baxter's behaviour, the marriage had indeed not been consummated, but that it had been sanctioned, or "approbated," in legalese. Thus, the marriage stood. An unhappy Mr. Baxter appealed then to the House of Lords.

The Lords pulled out such issues as *coitus interruptus* (or withdrawal before emission) and other methods of contraception. In their view, the institution of marriage was not necessarily for the procreation of children, nor are children the principal end of marriage. A marriage can be consummated even where children are not created. "It is the consent," they said, "whereby ariseth . . . the conjunction of bodies as well as minds."

But the difficulties in applying these principles are enormous. Taking judicial notice that the use of a sheath or condom is not the only method of contraception, the court stated its desire to avoid unnecessary detail on the topic. Then it went into detail. (Courts always do exactly the opposite of what they tell you they are going to do.) If the use of a sheath nullified a marriage, they said, then the rupture of a sheath in the course of a sexual act on a single occasion would mean that the marriage was consummated, though unwittingly and unintentionally.

Considerable deliberation led the Lords to decide that Parliament did not intend them to be involved in inquiries of this sort. Anyway, since other means of contraception are employed in a marriage without nullifying the marriage, neither should the use of the condom.

The word *consummate* was thus taken to mean what is understood in common social conditions — in other words, the act itself — and no further detail was entertained by the subject raised by Mr. Baxter in the appeal. That Mrs. Baxter consummated the marriage with Mr. Baxter with a condom was the principal of law "laid down" by the court.

Love Me, Love My Wife, Wife

Calvin Woodward was thirty-three years old when he met Christina. She was a student at the University of New Brunswick and Calvin was one of her professors. Inconveniently, Calvin was married to Barbara and the couple had a young son, Calvin Jr.

Calvin and Christina, who was twenty-one years old, "became involved." Christina took an apartment, and Calvin cohabited with her for several years. Thereafter they moved into several residences together, finally ending up in a house at Cameron Court, Fredericton, which they used as their permanent residence.

Meanwhile, Calvin and Barbara were divorced, and eventually Calvin married Christina. In due time they had a baby boy.

From the start, Calvin displayed a domineering personality, exercising an unusually strong influence and control over everyone he was involved with. During the first twelve years of their marriage, Christina was not permitted to associate either with her own friends and family or those of her husband.

In addition, Calvin insisted on the most unusual living arrangements. During their marriage, Calvin and Christina lived in their permanent residence at Cameron Court with his former wife Barbara and Calvin Jr. Though Barbara and her son had separate quarters and she carried on her own life, there were joint routine activities.

Christina put up with this for about eighteen years before the marriage finally deteriorated. Calvin had told her all along that the living arrangements were only temporary, but were necessary for financial and economic reasons. It had finally dawned on Christina that this was not true. Throughout all those years, particularly in the final period, Calvin preferred what some might consider unusual sexual practices. These were not acceptable to Christina. In the end, Calvin denied Christina any sexual relations, and all they did was argue.

It had taken eighteen years, but Christina finally petitioned for divorce on the grounds of mental cruelty based on Calvin's behaviour over the life of their marriage. She won. She was not buying Calvin's position of love me, love my wife, wife anymore.

Sex, Yes — But Not With My Husband

This is a very sad and painful case for Mr. Greenlees. His wife was eighteen years of age when they married, and he was older. During their honeymoon trip to Niagara Falls, he made repeated attempts to consummate the marriage, but she repelled all advances, all efforts by him to have sexual relations with her.

He was a patient fellow and fairly persistent, but over the three years they lived together he was not successful. On one occasion he even fastened her to the bed with ropes, but she broke the ropes and, not surprisingly, refused to submit to relations with him. Mrs. Greenlees, it seemed, had a real repugnance to the sexual act — with her husband.

Not, apparently, with everybody. Eventually she found employment with Mr. Kalinawski and gave birth to a child by him.

Since the marriage between Mr. and Mrs. Greenlees was never consummated, this union was declared annulled.

Nonetheless, let's give Mr. Greenlees an A for effort!

Patience Is a Virtue — But Seventeen Years?

Mr. Dredge and Ms. Harrison conceived a child and then decided to marry. Ms. Harrison was pregnant by Mr. Dredge when they went through the marriage ceremony, and a little over six months later their child was born.

After the ceremony, Mr. Dredge made every conceivable effort to consummate the marriage, but to no avail. At first, he believed that he was refused his conjugal rights because his wife did not want intercourse during the pregnancy. However, after the birth of the child, she still continued to refuse his advances. This case seems to be a variation of Mr. Greenlees's situation: Mr. Dredge was not repugnant to his wife prior to the marriage, but once the knot was tied, she cut him off.

Mr. Dredge gives new meaning to the word *patience.* He was a serving marine, and during the next eight years continued to make attempts to consummate the marriage between tours of duty. But after ten years, he decided that the marriage was over. He wanted to bring proceedings but found that it was too expensive for him. It wasn't until a further seven years had passed that he discovered that he could obtain financial assistance.

So, seventeen years after his marriage the court is asked by Mr. Dredge to grant a petition for nullity, meaning that the marriage never took place. But what about the child, now seventeen years old, who up to this date was a legitimate child of the marriage? If the decree by Mr. Dredge is granted, the inevitable consequence would be to change the status of the child to other than legitimate. Curious and unhappy though the consequence is, the fact that a child born after the marriage ceremony would suffer a change of status is not a ground to withhold a decree.

Though the court did wonder why the petitioner put off bringing the proceedings for so long, it accepted Mr. Dredge's evidence and reasons for wanting to annul his marriage, and found that he was candid and truthful. The marriage had not been consummated due to the wilful refusal of the wife to consummate it. The court granted Mr. Dredge's petition, though it regretted not being able to do anything to relieve the child from being placed in such an unfortunate position.

Whose Dress Is It, Anyway?

What is abnormal? The answer will depend on who you ask. When the court is the place that you seek the answer, the term *abnormal sex practices* takes on a different perspective. Some judges have decided that *coitus interruptus* can constitute mental cruelty and be grounds for divorce. Others have decided that a frail, sensitive, nervous wife forced to engage in fellatio against her wishes suffered mental cruelty. A husband's habit of reading "girlie" magazines and masturbating when he thought his wife was sleeping (she wasn't), though not behaviour his wife would accept, was not mentally cruel. However his actions in turning his wife over and refusing to look her in the face during intercourse *could* be considered cruel.

Where a husband, referred to by the court as G.G. (we'll call him G. Grant), borrows his wife's undergarments and clothes to the point where it becomes not merely an eccentricity, but a serious practice, the courts will carefully consider the behaviour. The issue that Mrs. I.G. (we'll call her Mrs. I. Grant) sought the court's assistance on was whether her husband's conduct was of a nature cruel enough to render intolerable future cohabitation with each other.

Perhaps in some circumstances the husband's practice of transvestism might not amount to cruelty of a degree that would entitle the wife to a divorce, but in the Grants' case, it has increased gradually in regularity and intensity over a period of years to the point where it causes continual stress to the wife and has brought about a separation.

Mrs. I. Grant did not wish to fight with her husband over which articles of her clothing would remain hers to use at which times. On more than one occasion she had found herself thinking, "whose dress is it anyway?" When Mr. Grant refused to change his behaviour pattern, or at least leave her clothing alone, she had had enough. Her health had been affected. It was intolerable to her to live with a man who preferred her Christian Diors to Armani suits.

The court takes pains to point out it is not its job to judge the parties, simply to say whether the grounds for divorce have been established. The court was pleased that the Grants did not fight over custody of the assets of the marriage, specifically the clothes, and granted Mrs. I. Grant her divorce decree based on G. Grant's transvestism.

Artificial Insemination —
Adultery or Not?

Now we'll look at two cases where the issue before the court is whether adultery is limited to the act of sexual congress, the conjunction of two human bodies, or whether the act is immaterial and the *result* can be called a form of adultery.

Mrs. Orford, married to Mr. Orford, has a child. The child, she says, is not fathered by Mr. Orford, but by a Mr. Hodgkinson, and she registers it as Mr. Hodgkinson's child. But, says Mrs. Orford, the child was conceived as a result of artificial insemination. This means that the suit for adultery brought against her by Mr. Orford is nonsense. Insemination or pregnancy without intercourse is not adultery. Mr. Orford's lawyers see it differently. They argue that the important element of adultery is the invasion of the marital rights of the offended party. A woman living with her husband who gives birth to a child by a man other than her husband by any means must be an adulteress.

There were no similar cases for the court to refer to, and after a vain search for them and a great deal of very difficult legal reasoning, the court decided that it really didn't need to decide the issue (whew!). It was discovered that, in fact, Mrs. Orford and Mr. Hodgkinson *had* indulged in sexual intercourse, and that the child had been conceived in a more normal way.

In light of recent medical advances in the field of reproduction, a question jumps to mind. Is a husband who deposits his sperm into a sperm bank — thereby "surrendering to another person his reproductive powers or faculties," in the words of the court — guilty of adultery?

Following the Orford case, a similar situation arose in Scotland.

Margaret Euphemia Shortland and Ronald George MacLennan were married but had lived apart for fourteen months when Margaret gave birth to a child. The two had not had marital relations, and Margaret claimed in answer to Ronald's charge of adultery that the child had been conceived by artificial insemination. She further claimed that Ronald had agreed to the process. Ronald denied this.

In Scotland, the law looks at the act and not the result, and in Ontario it is the result that is important. The court in Scotland asked: If the wife inserts the semen by herself, can it be argued that she is committing adultery by herself? If the semen comes from an unknown donor, can the woman commit adultery with a man she does not know and has never seen?

In this case, artificial insemination was held not to be adulterous because there was no conjunction of the wife's body with that of a man other than her husband.

Surprise ! I Just Got Sterilized !

Now lets make the leap from artificial insemination to the inability to fertilize.

Mr. and Mrs. Bravery had married young, he was twenty-five, she only twenty-one. Two years into their wedded bliss a son was born to them. Following the happy event, Mrs. Bravery frequently expressed her desire to have more children.

Just before their son's second birthday, Mrs. Bravery was shocked to discover that Mr. Bravery had undergone a sterilization operation. The reason for the operation, he claimed, was his wife's attitude toward their son. He said she saw the child not as a baby, but as a "showpiece," a toy who had to be perfectly dressed at all times.

Mr. Bravery, perhaps without realizing it, was apparently jealous of the place which the child held in his wife's affections. This jealousy was expressed in his desire not to give her any more children.

Both Mr. and Mrs. Bravery confirmed to the court that ever since the birth of their son, they had used contraceptives when having intercourse, and yet, Mr. Bravery had still had himself sterilized. Mrs. Bravery had never consented to the operation, had never even been approached by the surgeon for her feelings regarding the procedure. (Had the shoe been on the other foot, had Mrs. Bravery been the one being sterilized, you can bet that Mr. Bravery's feelings would have been considered.)

Though Mr. Bravery had told her beforehand what he was planning, she had not gone to the surgeon to protest. Mrs. Bravery was too astounded and upset to even discuss it, and she did not really think he would proceed with the operation. For some time after the operation Mrs. Bravery could not bear her husband even to be near her. She felt that he had become effeminate.

Although Mr. Bravery could have had his sterility reversed by another operation within a few years, he chose to become permanently sterile. It was this that finally caused the marriage to fall to pieces, and finally Mrs. Bravery left her husband.

She wanted a divorce and hoped that Mr. Bravery would start the proceedings. When he didn't, there was no alternative but for her to

start the action. At trial, Mrs. Bravery lost. She appealed the decision.

One judge of the Court of Appeal found that there was no just cause or excuse for Mr. Bravery's operation. It was an act which had disrupted the married state. Mrs. Bravery was the victim because the act was aimed at her to prevent her from having another child. One consequence of Mr. Bravery's sterilization was a deterioration in Mrs. Bravery's health. This judge pointed out that even had a young and inexperienced wife consented to her husband undergoing a sterilization operation, she should not be bound by that consent if in later years her health suffers on account of it.

The majority of the court did not agree, however, and they dismissed Mrs. Bravery's appeal. Though the operation had grave consequences on the marriage, in their opinion it did not amount to cruelty to the wife and was not grounds for divorce.

ALL ABOUT LOVE

He Says "I Do ": He Says "Me Too"

Whether in the brisk northern climate of Canada or south of the border, the courts appear to take judicial notice of the fundamental principle that "marriage is one of the basic civil rights of *man*."

In Manitoba, the Marriages Act provides that a minister may solemnize the ceremony of marriage between any two *persons*. Taking this to heart, Mr. North and his significant other delivered the required medical certificate to Mr. Matheson, the Registrar under the Vital Statistics Act. The banns declaring their intention to marry were published, and, in due time, the ceremony of marriage was solemnized in the presence of witnesses.

Before leaving on a honeymoon, the happy couple delivered all necessary documents to Mr. Matheson to exercise his administrative function and register the marriage. He refused, on the basis that Mr. North and his significant other were of the same sex. As a result, the newlyweds brought a court application to force him to register the marriage.

At this hearing, the court said marriage was more than a contract, it was an institution which created, beyond rights and obligations, the status of "husband" and "wife" for the participants. In view of this, sex is clearly an essential element of the relationship called marriage. It is and always has been recognized as the union of "man and woman."

This did not make either applicant too happy, since both men felt it was their basic civil right to marry each other should they so choose.

Sir Winston Churchill once said something to the effect that "man embraces woman," meaning that woman, having been created from the rib of man, in some way makes man both male and female. Here the court, skirting such complex thinking, resolved that only sexual opposites can attract the benefit of the state's recognition of their marriage.

Down in the State of Connecticut meanwhile, a bizarre law was passed prohibiting the use of contraceptives by married couples. Of course the only way to enforce such a law would be to have the condom police search the conjugal bedrooms for telltale signs of contraceptives. This was eventually found to violate the due process clause in the Fourteenth Amendment to the American Constitution and was therefore invalid.

On the other hand, when two members of the same sex attempted to marry in Connecticut, thereby challenging the law permitting only members of opposite sexes to marry, the law was upheld. It was decided that the law as it stood had nothing to do with the sex act between couples, but dealt only with a marital restriction.

Thus, it seems that in Connecticut, when the rights of opposite-sex couples are interfered with, it's against the Constitution, but it's fine for the State to step in and affect the status of same-sex couples.

I'll Marry You, I Promise

Never make the same mistake twice. We have all heard that before, and it's something we'll bet Sylvester Paddock and Catherine Robinson were sure to have been told. Did they listen? Do we?

There were really four people involved here, only two of them didn't realize it until later. There were Sly, Cathy, Mrs. Sly, and Mr. Cathy. That's right, Sly and Cathy were married to other people.

The two couples had performed their marriage vows in all sincerity, but Sly and Cathy were in a battle, were deeply at war with the best interests of social life. They were not only morally unfaithful to their marriage ties, they were quite prepared to make the same mistake twice. While still married to their respective and unknowing spouses, Sly and Cathy plighted their troth to each other — a neat trick, except that neither could carry through on the promised arrangement except on the demise or disappearance of Mrs. Sly or Mr. Cathy.

Now this is not a murder case; no one gets thrown from a train. But what a dilemma! In the end, it was too much for Sly, and the promised nuptials between Catherine and he never came off.

Catherine was not going to take this lying down, no sir! Mr. Sylvester Paddock was not going to get away with leading *her* down the bridal path and stopping short. She sued him straight away for breach of contract of promise of marriage. She hadn't been foolish enough to have gone out and purchased a wedding ensemble, but she would show him a thing or two.

Well, Sylvester lost at trial. The judge chose to see Catherine's side of the matter; Sylvester chose to appeal. Good thing, too, otherwise he might have had to go through with the promise or pay what it was worth to break it — a considerable sum of money we'd bet, given Catherine's obviously loving and gentle personality.

The Appeal Court did what it does best and reversed the trial judge's decision. Catherine, said the judges, had known all along of the existence of Mrs. Sly. It might have been a different matter had Sylvester led her astray by concealing the truth about his marital status. No innocent babes here!

Will Sylvester ever repeat his errant behaviour? Make the same mistake twice? Live dangerously and immorally? We would be willing to take bets on that one! If gambling were legal, that is.

Will You Love Me When I'm Old?

Well, you married me, didn't you? What did you expect: Rudolph Valentino, Clark Gable, Picasso? I worked all my life as a physician. I was seventy-six years old when we got married and you were sixty-one. I was a widower and you a widow. I had three grown children and you had four. For five months we slept in the same bed but now you insist we sleep in separate beds. Don't you love me?

Dr. Foster, in speaking to Mrs. Foster, didn't get very far. Almost one year to the day after she married the retired physician, she brought a court application in British Columbia to declare the marriage null and void, claiming that ever since the ceremony, Dr. Foster had failed to consummate the marriage. That, in fact, he is incapable of doing so because of his advanced age, and that his inability is permanent and incurable.

Dr. Foster and Mrs. Foster had lived together right up until a few days before the trial.

Dr. Foster was required by the court to undergo a medical examination, but he didn't show up, so the court had no choice but to accept Mrs. Foster's allegations. Poor Dr. Foster had lost his virility — something not unexpected in a man of his age.

The court could find no precedent stating that when an elderly man marries, his wife can get a decree of nullity of the marriage purely on the grounds of his physical inability to consummate the marriage. In fact, in different cases, courts have declined to proceed in suits where the parties are at an advanced period of life. Neither the court nor the public should have the annoyance of facing such suits to relieve the responsibilities and obligations of a person who ought to have exercised judgment at a much earlier time (for example, prior to the marriage).

Different considerations must apply to persons of advanced age than to those in the rosy flush of youth. The court said that Mrs. Foster should have known what she was getting when she got it. She should have decided before the marriage not to proceed because there was a distinct possibility that Dr. Foster's virility was not what it might be. The court was not prepared to grant a nullity decree, though consummation could not and would not take place.

Married Woman Sues Due to Sexual Solicitation

In an article written for the *Harvard Law Review*, then Chief Justice Magruder established what seems to be considered a well known phrase, "there is no harm in asking."

Under usual circumstances, he said, the court seems to agree that the solicitation to sexual intercourse could not be the subject of a lawsuit even though the person being asked might find the request offensive. It's not a "no-no." (Pardon the pun.)

An action will not exist in favour of a woman against a man who makes such a request, nor in favour of a man against a woman for such a solicitation.

However, there are circumstances surrounding solicitation which must also be considered.

For example, in one case, a Mr. Williamson sent a Mrs. Mitram obscene photographs of himself and repeatedly asked her to have illicit intercourse with him. This could be actionable.

In another case, Marcia Samms, a respectable married woman, had never once encouraged David Eccles's attentions in any way. She had, in fact, repulsed his advances. Nonetheless, over a period of eight months, Mr. Eccles persisted in calling Marcia by phone at all hours, even late at night, and asking her to have illicit sexual relations with him. On one occasion, he even boldly came to her residence to ask her to engage in relations with him. At that time, he made an indecent exposure of his person.

Marcia found all this insulting, indecent, and obscene. David had deeply wounded her feelings, and, as a result of his behaviour, though he never once put a hand on her, she suffered great anxiety and fear for her personal safety. She also suffered intense emotional stress.

She sued David for damages for this distress and for punitive damages. She lost and appealed.

The situation described is clearly different from that intended by Chief Justice Magruder. The trial court that dismissed Marcia's action was wrong to do so and was reversed in favour of Marcia.

Are You a Boy or Are You a Girl?

We deal here with the only case reference in Ontario of a transsexual change from female to male. There are cases of males changing to females by way of sex reassignment surgery, but this case is quite unique.

To protect the privacy of the parties, their children and grandchildren, let's call the people involved Ava and Betty.

Ava and Betty were both born female. Ava had a normal adolescence, eventually married and had children. Betty, while anatomically female, developed discomfort and a desire to possess the body of a man. She did not identify with women or behave as a woman most of her life. However, she did get married and had a child. Just after the child's birth, she and her husband separated.

Ava and Betty met. Ava learned that Betty thought of herself as a man trapped inside a woman's body, and that she wanted to become a man.

Several months after meeting Ava, Betty moved into the basement apartment in the home of Ava, her husband, and her children. Betty soon started wearing men's clothes around the house.

Next, Betty began sex reassignment and gender reorientation therapy. She began taking long-term male hormone (testosterone) therapy, administering one injection to herself per month. The result was a redistribution of her body fat, and an increased growth in facial and body hair. Menstruation stopped and her breasts shrunk.

After about a year, Betty had the outward appearance of a male, and she began female-to-male surgery. She had her breasts removed and her chest reconstructed in a male chest contour. She had a pan-hysterectomy, the removal of her uterus, fallopian tubes, and ovaries.

Ava and her husband separated, and some time after that a relationship started between Ava and Betty. This relationship continued for twenty-odd years before it ended, and Ava and Betty decided to separate.

Betty throughout the relationship had played the male role and appeared as such to the children and grandchildren. During the

period of time that Ava and Betty resided together as "man and wife," they accumulated substantial mutual assets, all however under legal title of Ava.

Betty brought an application under the Family Law Act for support from Ava. Unfortunately, in order to be entitled to support, Betty had to come under the definition of "man" in the Family Law Act. When the case came to court, the issue was whether Betty could be defined as a man.

There are numerous cases to refer to where a male has become a female by way of sex reassignment surgery. The subject then is physically and psychologically capable of sexual activity as a woman, and her husband has been obliged to support her as his wife. There are, however, no decisions to fall back on where a female has changed to a male.

The fact that to the outside world Betty and Ava appeared to be man and wife was not enough. That Betty could (and did) apply under the Vital Statistics Act to change her birth certificate from female to male is not enough. The section contemplates not a psychological change but an actual radical anatomical change.

A total hysterectomy is considered by most women to be a radical anatomical change, but because Betty's external genitalia had not been touched surgically, the law logically enough didn't consider it sufficiently radical. If Betty had stopped taking hormones, her body would have physically changed back to more female outlines. In that case, had her birth certificate been altered, Betty would be in the position of a legal male with a female body.

While there could be a change of sex that creates the legal basis of a Family Law Act claim, the change must be irreversible after surgery is completed. Under these conditions, Betty is not within the definition of "man" under the Act and cannot get support from Ava. Betty can pursue Ava for an interest in the assets they had accumulated, but she must do so on the basis of Trust Law, that Ava holds a share for Betty, not on the basis of the Family Law as a spouse.

This case decided that the transsexual change must affect the sexual organs through irreversible and radical surgery before the spousal status can be achieved.

In the Arms of Another Man

Somewhere in Queensland, Australia, one day, Mr. Connolly just happened past the Southport Hotel. As chance would have it he discovered that his wife had retired with Mr. White to a room in the hotel. Further research revealed his wife and Mr. White in an intimate embrace in a bed in the room.

Mr. Connolly, it seems, was of a passionate nature, and, being provoked by what he saw, he caused a good deal of physical pain and some suffering to Mr. White. That unfortunate soul needed medical treatment and subsequently sued Mr. Connolly for damages for the injuries he had sustained, taking the position that an assault is unlawful and provocation is not a defence. Mr. Connolly defended the action in part by claiming that the force he had used was necessary to prevent the repetition of the act or insult that had originally provoked him to assault Mr. White. He also indicated that the force used was not intended to cause death or grievous bodily harm.

The court decided that the law regards assault as an offence unless it is authorized or justified or excused by law. In the circumstances, the court viewed provocation as a possible excuse for assault in a civil action such as the one launched by Mr. White. Mr. Connolly could therefore now raise it as a defence and try to rely on it.

And what of Mrs Connolly? The records don't show whether Mr. Connolly's show of manly strength brought her back to the haven of his arms or whether she still preferred the charms of the battered Mr. White. Whoever she chose to bestow her favours upon, however, they were most certainly not bestowed in the vicinity of the Southport Hotel.

Poison Him, Then Sue Him

Laura and Arthur Imperadeiro married in their home village in Portugal and had three children. The family moved to Ontario, Canada, and shortly thereafter, in 1961, Laura and Arthur separated from each other. Laura moved in with Arthur's brother, Abilio, as his housekeeper. They live under the same roof, but both deny any sexual contact. She is, she claims, Abilio's housekeeper and nothing more.

Eventually Laura, Abilio, and the children moved to Vancouver and became part of the Portuguese community there.

One day, in 1961, shortly before the separation, George, Laura's second-oldest son, had come home with a policeman and accused his mother and his Uncle Abilio of trying to poison his father. Now, years later, word of the alleged plot to poison Arthur spread like wildfire throughout Vancouver's Portuguese community.

Eventually, they learned that Arthur himself had been the source of the allegations. In a scribbler, he had written the following extracts, and had then passed the scribbler around to other family members: "If I wanted, now, I could put them in jail . . . I want to see them in this country in such misery that even the dogs will be afraid of them!

"The police asked me if I wanted them picked up. I said no; he was my brother and she was my wife. . . . After a week the Chief of Police came to see me and asked me if I wanted to have them arrested. I was very lucky not to have drunk the wine because the wine had something poisonous.

"Degenerate! Trying to put an end to my life! But God is powerful, and it is them who will be taken by the devil. And it wouldn't take too long!"

Arthur had made no attempt to justify the clearly libelous statements, nor did he tender an apology. Laura and Abilio denied any attempt to poison him, but the flying rumours forced them to move to the interior of the province. Not only that, but they were ostracized by members of their family. Neither George nor his sister Agostinna will have anything further to do with their mother. Laura's parents refuse to correspond with her. Laura has had to seek medical attention for the emotional trauma arising from the situation.

Section 13 of the Married Woman's Property Act provides in part that no husband or wife is entitled to sue the other for a tort. No action would be available to Laura during the existence of her marriage to Arthur. However, after divorce or annulment a woman is not barred from bringing an action to recover for injuries during the marriage. Although Laura and Arthur were still married technically at the time of the wrong-doing, after the marriage was dissolved, Laura was able to sue. Laura and Abilio each received a damage award against Arthur as well as exemplary damages (as a punishment) and their legal costs.

As for Arthur, his soul was poisoned by what he perceived as a slight by his wife and brother, and then — insult to injury — they sued him.

POOR SOCIAL SKILLS CASES

Fig Your Love

I asked the witch doctor,
He told me what to do,
I asked the witch doctor,
He said just what to do

"The Witch Doctor," a popular song of the 1960s

Mr. Stratton and a friend acquired from some nameless source "love powders," represented by the nameless source to be perfectly harmless but extremely efficacious. The intention was to secretly administer these "love powders" to two young women with whom they were friendly. The young ladies' sexual passions would be sufficiently excited that they would find Mr. Stratton and his friend completely irresistible.

The two gentlemen called on the young women and during their visit offered them some figs. The young ladies ate the figs, having no reason to suppose they were tainted in any way. However, the figs had been liberally imbued with Mr. Stratton's "love powders." Mr. Stratton appears to have been wildly misled about the power of the powders. Not only did they not have the expected reaction, but several hours later both women became quite sick and suffered severe pain for hours thereafter.

Investigation revealed that one of the ingredients of these powders was cantharides, or "Spanish Fly," a concoction of dried, crushed blister beetles long reputed to be a sexual stimulant, but which is actually an irritant.

Mr. Stratton was charged with assault. Though he was ignorant of the actual effects to be expected of the drug he administered, he knew it was not ordinary food and he induced and deceived the young women into taking it without their conscious consent. This deceit was equivalent to Mr. Stratton using force and overpowering the young ladies. The court compared it to a person being handed an explosive by someone who misrepresents or conceals its dangerous qualities. That explosive then explodes in that person's pocket. In this case, the drug exploded in the young women's stomachs. The court was quick to say that although one example is external and the other internal, that does not matter, the result is similar.

Mr. Stratton's approach to dating was found to be more than undesirable, it was a criminal act — assault and battery. The moral? When you "date," do not "fig" your love.

If I Lose, I'll Spit in Your Face

William E. Alcorn, who hailed from Jasper County, Illinois, brought an action for trespassing against Andrew J. Mitchell. Although the matter had not yet been decided (the judge reserving judgment until a later date), at the close of the trial, the court adjourned.

Well, Mr. Alcorn was incensed — he was beside himself. Sensing somehow that he had lost his case, he decided that justice had not been served swiftly enough to temper his sensibilities. He wasn't going to be patient, he was not going to take this lying down, no sir! What could he do to show his rage? What insult could he convey to the defendant, who to his mind seemed to be gloating?

Immediately upon the adjournment being announced, in the presence of a large number of people in the courtroom, Mr. Alcorn deliberately strode up to Mr. Mitchell, who turned to greet him. Mr. Alcorn inhaled, coughed deeply, and spat into the face of his opponent. Mr. Mitchell stood stunned as spittle dripped down his face.

This action by Mr. Alcorn was both highly provocative and akin to retaliation by force. Mr. Mitchell felt compelled to respond in kind. The affair could have degenerated into a sort of trial by spitting, but Mr. Mitchell restrained himself and launched into a more fervent lawsuit than he had been defending. He sued Mr. Alcorn (a wealthy man) for redress (or a towel) and punitive damages (asking the court to do what parents did before raising children was a science — send Mr. Alcorn to his room as a punishment, only instead of his room, the court would send Mr. Alcorn to his bank account).

To preserve "the public tranquillity" and to discourage Mr. Mitchell from resorting to personal violence on the person of Mr. Alcorn as a means of redress, the court enthusiastically provided substantial protection for the outrage the complainant had suffered.

The court, in setting out its position in society (and how it perceived itself), stated: "Suitors, in the assertion of their rights, should be allowed approach to the *temple of justice* without incurring there exposure to such disgraceful indignities. . . ." In this case, the jury was instructed to give "vindictive" damages, as Mr. Alcorn's actions were "malicious, wilful, wanton, and an

outrageous indignity." He had indulged his feelings for the purpose of insult, and, because he was a wealthy man, it was felt by the court that he had not been made to pay too dearly for that indulgence.

The lower court judgment was affirmed and Mr. Alcorn lost . . . again. Next time, Sir, try a spittoon.

The Human Shield

This case is remarkable for, if nothing else, the number of times it was heard. Back in 1891, it went through four trials and subsequent appeals. What was the fuss? Let's look.

It was early on an ordinary winter afternoon in the offices occupied by Mr. Russell Sage's company. Mr. Sage was a very rich man, owner of railroads, dealer in stocks, director of banks. Did this have anything to do with William Laidlaw, Jr.'s persistence in litigation? At this date, who can say? But stranger things have happened.

Mr. Laidlaw, bearing a letter of introduction from no less a luminary than Mr. Rockefeller, called in to see Mr. Sage about some railroad bonds. Mr. Sage, when told this, stepped from his private office into the anteroom and up to a window which looked out onto the lobby where Mr. Laidlaw waited.

Also waiting, on a settee, was another gentlemen, a Mr. Norcross. As he opened the door to usher Mr. Laidlaw into the anteroom, Mr. Sage spoke to Mr. Norcross. This gentleman immediately arose and, carrying a carpet bag in his left hand, walked over and handed Mr. Sage a note. Mr. Sage found it necessary to read the note twice. Perhaps he was unable to believe the contents. It read: "The bag I hold in my hand contains ten pounds of dynamite. . . . I demand $1,200,000, or I will drop the bag. Will you give it? Yes or no?"

Mr. Laidlaw, unaware of the drama unfolding in the lobby, had meanwhile walked over to a large table in the centre of the anteroom where he stood facing the windows which looked out onto the street. In front of those windows, busily reading the tape that spilled from the ticker machine, stood a clerk, Mr. Norton. To these two gentlemen, an ordinary day was going its ordinary way. How could they know that out in the lobby, playing for time, Mr. Sage had carefully folded the note and handed it back to Mr. Norcross, saying that he had an appointment right then. Perhaps Mr. Norcross could come back later in the day?

It's not hard to imagine Mr. Norcross's disbelief. "Then, do I understand you to refuse my offer?" he asked.

Mr. Sage replied, "Oh no, I don't refuse your offer. I have an appointment with two gentlemen. I think I can get through with them in about two minutes, and then I will see you."

Norcross, still clutching the fateful carpet bag, began to back towards the main door. As he did this, Mr. Sage was also backing up — towards the desk in the anteroom beside which stood Mr. Laidlaw. When he reached the table he perched on one corner of it. And here's where the nut of our case lies.

Mr. Laidlaw claimed that Sage had taken his hand and gently moved him to stand in front of him, between Sage and Norcross, deliberately to use his body as a human shield if Mr. Norcross's threat should prove true. Mr. Sage, of course, denied this.

At the threshold, Mr. Norcross stopped, looked at Mr. Sage, and asked once again if his offer was being refused.

Not so, reiterated Mr. Sage, he had an appointment which he would get through in two minutes, and he would then see Norcross.

Norcross stepped to one side and dropped the bag. There was a flash and a crashing explosion, and then nothing but the sound of timbers, plaster, and dust settling.

Everything in the office was wrecked. The partitions, floors, joists, plaster, desks, tables, chairs, and other furnishings were all destroyed. The windows and window frames were blown out, and a locked steel safe in an adjoining room was blown open, its contents scattered.

It was a miracle that anybody in the office survived. Not one person escaped uninjured. Mr. Norcross was blown to pieces and the luckless ticker-tape reader, Mr. Norton, was blown through the window to his death.

As the dust cleared Laidlaw and Sage were lying together, both having sustained damage. Mr. Sage had to lift Mr. Laidlaw off him, the first time, in his testimony, that he had laid hands upon him. Mr. Laidlaw had injured hands and had been struck by "missiles" in his midsection. As time unfolded, it would be found that his memory had been impaired by the blast. He was unable to remember what he was told to do from one day to the next.

This was one of the things that swayed the final court to hear this case away from believing that Mr. Laidlaw had in fact been used as a human shield. That, and the fact that "missiles" were found in the front of his body, although he claimed to have been facing Mr. Sage, and that his hands were damaged although he claimed that Mr. Sage had been holding one of them in his own two hands.

Even if Mr. Laidlaw had been used as a shield, said the court, judgment could not be given in his favour. All his injuries were caused by Norcross's act — exploding the dynamite. Had there been no explosion, Laidlaw would not have been hurt. Given the intensity of the explosion, Sage's alleged action in moving Laidlaw a short distance from where he was standing would not have caused him to suffer any greater harm than he would have suffered anyway.

Although the court felt sympathy for poor Mr. Laidlaw, they decided that "every proper consideration requires us to disregard our sympathy, and decide the questions of law presented according to the well-established rules governing them."

This judgment was passed in 1899 — almost eight years after the explosion took place. The wheels of justice apparently ground exceedingly slowly even then.

The Serrated Guest

For four years in the 1940s Ella Blakeley and her husband and Martin Shortal and his wife lived on adjoining farms in Jefferson County, Iowa. Martin and his wife eventually separated and divorced, and about six months later Martin sold off a portion of his farm. He planned to live in his house on the other part.

Ella and her husband stayed on good terms with Martin. One evening just after the sale, Martin came to visit the Blakeley home. It was raining hard and he was soaking wet and his clothes were muddy. He wanted to stay all night. The Blakeleys, feeling sorry for him, provided him with a bed. In the morning, the three had breakfast and then Martin, Ella, and her husband sat around visiting until about noon, when the Blakeleys went to town, leaving Martin alone in their house.

The couple came home around 4:00 PM, and Ella started to enter the kitchen. She pushed the door partly open and saw Martin lying on the floor with pools of blood about him. She screamed, "Oh, my God, Martin has killed himself!" and began to faint. Luckily, her husband, standing behind her, prevented her fall.

The Blakeleys at once drove to a neighbour's and called the sheriff and the coroner. These officials came about an hour later (Jefferson County was very rural in the 1940s) and found Martin dead in the kitchen. His throat had been cut and there was a great deal of blood on the floor and about the room. By his side lay a blood-stained skinning knife.

As a result of her discovery, Ella had to be treated by a doctor for nervous shock. Since that time, she had had difficulty sleeping and was nervous and restless. She could not return to her home for some time after the event.

The fact that Martin Shortal committed suicide in Ella's home was not the basis of Ella's lawsuit against Martin's estate. It was the injury to Ella, the nervous shock that resulted, for which she sought to be compensated.

The court found that each case must be decided on its own facts. In committing the act of suicide Martin was what the court called a "wilful wrongdoer. . . . He failed to act properly in the premises . . .

the gory and ghastly sight confronting [Ella] caused a shock and that shock was the . . . result of his wrongful act."

Ella's action arose before Martin's death and survived it. The serrated guest's estate was found responsible to pay for the injury Ella had suffered.

This was neither the best way to distribute an estate nor, certainly, the way one would want a guest in one's home to leave it. Martin was obviously very distraught and irrational. His act did not give Ella the right to part of his estate. It was the result of his act as it affected Ella that gave her the right.

I Am a Blabber Mouth

T here are days in our lives when rolling over and going back to sleep would be the most appropriate thing we could do. This, alas, is something very few of us ever do. The next best thing would be to keep our thoughts to ourselves, a lesson that Eugene William Mathe learned the hard way.

At about 10:15 AM on a nice September day, Eugene entered the Canada Trust Company on Douglas Street in beautiful Victoria, British Columbia. He stepped up to the wicket where Kathleen Hadley was a teller. Within the hearing of other people in the immediate area, Eugene announced, "I have a .38 in my pocket, hand over the cash."

Kathleen went to her cash drawer and started getting out twenties. At the same time she set off the silent alarm. When she handed Eugene the twenties, he said, "That's not what I want." He then said that he was only joking, that he himself was a security guard, and that he did not want the cash. He shook Kathleen's hand and left, going north on Douglas Street with another customer of the bank.

At 11:10 AM Eugene was arrested near the fountain at Centennial Square by Constable Dibden. Constable Dibden asked Eugene to accompany him to the police station a couple of blocks away. Eugene agreed to go along, and on the way, in response to Constable Dibden's questions, he said that yes, he had been at the Canada Trust, and well, yes, he had told Kathleen that he was staging a hold-up, but really, Officer, he was only fooling. He didn't *mean* to hold up the place.

At the station, Eugene was turned over to Detective Horsman who observed that while Eugene had obviously been drinking, he did not appear to be intoxicated.

Eugene was charged with attempted robbery and warned of his rights.

At his trial, Eugene did not testify. He was convicted. Even though he insisted he had been joking, and though he did not take the money, the trial judge decided that Eugene had just got cold feet, he'd had a change of heart.

Eugene appealed his conviction. Mr. Justice MacLean of the Court of Appeal decided that although Eugene's words and actions could have been interpreted the way the trial judge saw them, they could

just as easily be explained the way Eugene explained them — he stupidly went into the bank and uttered his words as a joke. If, in fact, the transaction were a joke, there was no crime. If on the other hand, Eugene had been serious initially but had decided to abandon the transaction, then there was a crime.

Since the possibility of innocence existed, there could not be the required proof of crime beyond a reasonable doubt. Eugene's conviction was quashed and a verdict of acquittal entered. He got off . . . this time, but not without a lot of aggravation and a large legal bill. You don't go to the appeal court for free.

Yep, next time Eugene will probably keep his jokes to himself.

LAWYERS AND JUDGES

It Takes Two Justices to
Try a Cow

Robert Headrick, a farmer who lived at Red Deer Hill in the District of Kinistino in the Province of Saskatchewan, appeared before two of Her Majesty's Justices of the Peace for his district, expressing great concern for his cattle. Robert's fear centred on a certain red-and-white cow — not his, but chewing its cud in proximity to his herd. In Robert's opinion this cow was not a well cow, and he feared that it might cause his cattle to become diseased. Robert therefore filed a complaint under oath against the cow.

After reasonable inquiry, the two justices could find no owner for the accused cow. Further, after a thorough examination by the two justices, the accused cow, which had a large lump on its jaw and a fetid discharge, was declared to be diseased.

In accordance with Form "C" of the Northwest Ordinance, the justices ordered the destruction of the cow, charging a fee for examination and a fee for mileage and destruction. They issued a document to this effect under seal and stated that the conviction would be good and effectual for all intents and purposes.

The fervent wish of those who reviewed this legal process was that these justices limit themselves in the future to cows.

The Evidence
That Wouldn't Stand Up

Lamar Manus of Nicholas, Georgia, was accused of attacking a fifteen-year-old boy. The boy gave evidence that his assailant was circumcised.

Using the seize-the-bull-by-the-horns defence, lawyer David Montgomery sought permission of the court to have his client's penis admitted into evidence so that the court could compare it with the victim's description.

Initially, Mr. Montgomery suggested that Mr. Manus be displayed behind closed doors to the prosecutor. This suggestion, however, met with a cold reception, and eventually the courtroom was cleared and Mr. Manus had the opportunity to display his uncircumcised penis to a jury of nine men and three women. Following this, it took them two hours to come back with a Not Guilty verdict. Obviously, the probative value of the evidence took time to sink in. Of considerable interest is the fact that Mr. Manus did in a courtroom what would have been a criminal offence had he done it outside one.

This type of evidence doesn't always "stand up in court," for a Florida judge refused a similar request to admit an accused's penis into evidence. Nor would he accept photographs or a wooden model of the organ. In his opinion, it was of little evidential value.

The Case of the Kissing Judge

Alberto O. Miera, Jr., sat as a Minnesota District Judge. Neil Johnson was a court reporter. Mr. Johnson alleged that Judge Miera had made advances of a sexual nature to him in the past. He now took Judge Miera to task for an incident that he claimed had occurred in the judge's chambers.

On this occasion, Mr. Johnson told Judge Miera that he "just wanted to do his job and did not want to clash any more." This apparently inspired Judge Miera to get up from his desk, stride past Mr. Johnson, and suddenly, without warning, turn and plant a kiss on Mr. Johnson's lips. With that he stated, "Oh! We clashed."

Judge Miera was publicly disciplined for misconduct and suspended without pay for one year.

Though the judge denied that he ever kissed Mr. Johnson, in 1986 a jury decided that such was not the case and awarded the court reporter $375,000. On appeal, the damage award was reduced to $122,000.

Though Judge Miera returned to the bench in July 1989, he did not run for re-election in 1990. He now practises law and has said, "I didn't kiss him as he said. I said that from the beginning and I'll say it again now."

Judge Miera has filed for bankruptcy. The question now is, can he avoid paying Mr. Johnson the $122,000 judgment?

The United States Bankruptcy Code establishes that people who file for bankruptcy are not relieved from debts caused by "wilful and malicious injury." The United States Circuit Court of Appeals panel upheld a ruling by a District Court Judge in St. Paul, stating that the court judgment against Mr. (formerly Judge) Miera could not be discharged in his bankruptcy case because the kiss was a "wilful and malicious injury."

The "kissing judge" could not escape judgment.

The Legal Merry-Go-Round

Be honest! How many of you (unless you are either a member of one of the professions or married to someone who is) actually like doctors or lawyers?

The truth is, we lawyers are not all bad, and many of us are quite civilized. Sometimes, however, when logic gives way to emotion, like anyone else in our world, we can get a little childish. This can result in an amusing trip to the "legal merry-go-round."

Harry A. Burglass, a lawyer, brought a medical malpractice action against Dr. Rowena Spencer in Jefferson, Lousiana, on behalf of his clients. Mr. Burglass did not interview his witnesses prior to the trial, nor did he obtain competent medical advice in relation to the case. In view of this, the lawsuit was not successful.

Dr. Spencer, in tune with the current trend in society, sued Mr. Burglass, seeking damages from him for embarrassment, discomfort, and lost time resulting from the court action orchestrated by the lawyer for his clients.

When Judge Floyd W. Newlin dismissed Dr. Spencer's lawsuit, she appealed. In the Court of Appeal, Judge Schott held that Dr. Spencer's allegation that the lawyer had "frivolously" filed the lawsuit did not amount to proof of malice or malicious prosecution on his part. Though he could be sued by his own client, were he negligent, that did not help her. The original suit had been filed by the lawyer at the behest and on behalf of his clients, Stephen Lester Parker and Adam Parker, and not on his own behalf. Even had he realized that his clients had no case, he violated no duty to the doctor by not withdrawing the lawsuit. The Court of Appeal dismissed Dr. Spencer's appeal.

We understand that Mr. Burglass, not to be outdone, launched a final strike at Dr. Spencer for having maliciously prosecuted him. And the beat goes on . . .

Pants That Kill

In Sussex, England, in the 1830s, a man was tried for stealing from a residence a pair of leather pants. He was found guilty by a jury.

The law at the time required a very heavy penalty — capital punishment. The members of the jury were horrified and quickly asked whether they would be permitted to change their verdict. That the verdict had been duly arrived at and delivered prevented such a course of action. The clerk of the court did, however, advise the jury that there was nothing to prevent them from adding to their verdict.

The jury immediately and unanimously joined to their finding of "guilty" the words "of manslaughter." This crime was selected as it gave the judge wide discretion as to how he could sentence the accused.

In any event the court record reflected that a man tried for stealing leather pants was found guilty of manslaughter.

The Defence Rests

Eddie G. Javor was up on two counts of an indictment charging possession and sale of heroin. He was one of three defendants and he was looking at a seven-year jail term.

Eddie retained a trial attorney by the name of Samuel S. Brody. There is always a question of competence when hiring an attorney, especially in such circumstances as Eddie now found himself, and one's own trial is not the proving ground that, especially, perhaps, anyone in the position of the defendant, would appreciate using to test an attorney's ability or competency.

Mr. Brody apparently found Eddie extremely boring, his case of little merit and challenge, or else he had that sleeping sickness called narcolepsy. There are other possible explanations, but we'll never really know, because unfortunately Mr. Brody died sometime after the trial, and the cause remains somewhat of a mystery.

The fact remains that throughout the trial Mr. Brody was often sound asleep or dozing. This did not help Eddie, particularly during those portions of the trial when very relevant evidence was given to help the prosecution's case.

Mr. Brody failed to observe witnesses, listen to testimony, pose objections, cross-examine witnesses, enter rebuttal evidence, or prepare any legal arguments that might have been proper or helpful to Eddie. This, thank goodness, is pretty rare conduct for a defence lawyer.

As might be surmised, Eddie was convicted, got seven years, and appealed, among other applications. His petition was referred to the Honourable Ralph J. Giffen, United States Magistrate, who held evidentiary hearings and concluded that: "though petitioner had not received the competent assistance of his counsel, he failed to show that prejudice resulted."

The District Court adapted the magistrate's position and Eddie appealed again. By this time, Eddie was not in custody, having completed service of his sentence. The United States Court of Appeals, Ninth Circuit, ordered a new evidentiary hearing to determine whether any prejudice resulted to Eddie based on his attorney's action, or lack of actions, at his trial. It was decided that "today we conclude that when an attorney for a criminal defendant sleeps through a substantial portion of a trial, such conduct is inherently prejudicial and thus no separate showing of prejudice is necessary."

Eddie's right to counsel was violated not because of specific legal errors or omissions indicating incompetence, but because he had *no* legal assistance during a substantial portion of his trial. "Prejudice," the court said, is inherent in this case because an unconscious or sleeping counsel is equivalent to no counsel at all." The trial judge noted that Eddie's attorney was often dozing and that other attorneys nudged and kicked him in an effort to wake him up.

Even though Eddie had served his sentence, the collateral consequences of his conviction for sale and possession of heroin continue. The decision was reversed.

HOUSE CALLS
WOULD BE SAFER

The Surgeon Juggler

Most people have a deep-rooted and understandable fear of leaving a hospital with fewer body parts than they went in with. Fifty-two-year-old Mr. Marshall of Nova Scotia was no exception.

Mr. Marshall had been a sea-faring man since he was sixteen. About thirty years earlier, he had fallen from the foremast of a barque some forty-five feet to the deck, seriously injuring himself. He lost all sensation down the backs of his legs, around his buttocks, and in some muscles of his feet. He was, to a degree, permanently disabled, but now was suffering considerable discomfort, and found himself referred to Dr. Curry, a distinguished surgeon of high standing in Halifax.

Dr. Curry's examination revealed paralysis of the bowel and a septic bladder. Internally, Mr. Marshall was not in good shape at all. He was admitted to Victoria General Hospital and not discharged until about six weeks later.

Three months later he returned to Victoria General, was treated and released.

Over the next eight years, poor Mr. Marshall suffered almost constantly from fever, headache, dry tongue, sinus infections, and general septic poisoning, as well as a severe pain in his left loin diagnosed as a hernia. He was in and out of the hospital several times during this period.

Eventually, Dr. Curry found an abscess in the area of Mr. Marshall's left kidney necessitating a six-month spell in hospital. Finally, Mr. Marshall told Dr. Curry he wanted the hernia cured. After examining him again, Dr. Curry said, "All right," and the operation took place.

A day or two later Mr. Marshall was advised by Dr. Curry that his left testicle had been removed because "it might have caused trouble."More than a little upset, Mr. Marshall said he had never given his consent to that course of action, in fact, had not been advised that it was necessary.

Mr. Marshall's lawyer, J. J. Power, issued the court action. The claim alleged that Dr. Curry was negligent in diagnosing the case and in not informing Mr. Marshall that it might be necessary when treating the hernia to remove the testicle. It also stated that removing the testicle in the circumstances constituted an assault by Dr. Curry on Mr. Marshall.

L. A. Lovett, representing Dr. Curry, posited that removal of the testicle was a necessary part of the operation to cure the hernia, and that the necessity for doing so could not be determined before the operation.

It seems that poor Mr. Marshall could not afford to hire expert "gunfighter" witnesses. His Honour Chief Justice Chisholm pointed out that Dr. Curry called "three eminent surgeons to support the propriety of his procedure." These experts concluded that the defendant performed "good surgery," and the court concluded as a result that there can be no negligence if the surgery was good surgery.

This left the question of the assault — bringing about a harmful contact without the consent of the other party.

The court found as fact that there was neither express consent by Mr. Marshall, *nor* implied consent. However, since Mr. Marshall failed to provide his own experts, Dr. Curry's evidence — that removal of the testicle was necessary for the protection of Mr. Marshall's health and possibly his life — was accepted.

The court went further in stating: "Every human being of adult years and sound mind has a right to determine what shall be done with his own body . . . a surgeon who performs an operation without his patient's consent commits an assault, for which he is liable in damages. This is true except in cases of emergency. . . . If an operation is forbidden by a patient, consent is not to be implied. Silence does not give consent."

Performing "good surgery," it appears, cannot be taken as the *right* to operate. However, if you are able to (pardon the pun) *marshal* your expert evidence and establish an emergency, it seems that you as a physician will not be exposed to legal liability.

Chief Justice Chisholm made reference to two factors which would not mean much to any of us. Firstly, "the defendant is a surgeon of high standing," and secondly, "the plaintiff has never been married."

It leaves us to ponder: if Mr. Marshall had been married and of high standing, and if Dr. Curry had not been married or of lesser standing, would the case of the surgeon juggler have been performed differently?

The Student Lab Animal

When you hear the words *surgical assault* you might imagine Jack Nicholson acting the role of a deranged surgeon; you might conjure up an image of something only a little less sinister than the Island of Dr. Moreau and vivisection. Reality is much more mundane.

Dr. G. M. Wyant was professor of anaesthetics and chief of that department at the University of Saskatchewan Hospital during the 1960s. His co-defendant, Dr. J. E. Merriman, also a medical practitioner, was director of the cardio-pulmonary laboratory. Wyant and Merriman conducted and carried out medical research projects, some of which involved the comparative study of anaesthetics. To get volunteers for those experiments, the doctors utilized the university employment office.

Walter Halushka, age twenty-one, attending summer school at the university, went to the employment office to find a job. He was advised that although there was no work available, he could earn fifty dollars if he wanted to be the subject of a test at the University Hospital. He was told that it would last a couple of hours, that it was a "safe test," and that there was nothing to worry about.

Walter went to the anaesthesia department at the hospital and met with Dr. Wyant. He was told that they would be testing a new drug on him and that electrodes would be put in both arms, both legs and his head. He was assured that it was a perfectly safe test that had been conducted many times before. Instrument hook-up would take about one hour, and the test itself would take about five hours. On completion, Walter would get to sleep, he would be fed, then he would receive fifty dollars and be driven home.

Doctor Wyant also told Walter that an incision would be made in his left arm to allow a catheter or tube to be inserted into his vein.

Walter agreed to be the test subject and was asked to sign a form of consent, stating, in part, that "the test to be undertaken in connection with this study has been explained to me and I understand fully what is proposed to be done." The form went on to release all parties conducting the study, the hospital and university from "all responsibility and claims for . . . effects or accidents."

Walter skimmed the form, picked out the word *accident*, and asked the

doctor what this meant. The example he got was "falling down the stairs at home after the test."

Of course the intention was to release all responsibility on the part of the experimenters for injury before, during or after the test, whether physical, medical or whatever.

From hereon we understand the maxim, *caveat emptor*, "let the buyer beware." Loosely applied, you must make your own diligent inquiry and ask, ask, ask. We can only speculate that at some point, accurate information would have been forthcoming to Walter. Getting a second unbiased opinion does not hurt either.

The new anaesthetic (commercially called "Fluoromar") had not been previously used or tested by Doctors Wyant and Merriman in any way.

The procedure described to Walter was followed, save for one fact: the catheter was not merely inserted into his vein, but was advanced towards his heart. When the catheter reached the vicinity of the heart, he experienced discomfort. The anaesthetic was then administered to him. Later, the catheter tip was advanced through the various heart chambers out into the pulmonary artery.

Walter eventually fell into deep anaesthesia. A short time later his cardiac rhythm suggested the level of anaesthesia was too deep, so it was decreased. He then suffered a complete cardiac arrest.

Immediate steps were taken to resuscitate his heart by manual massage. To reach his heart an incision was made from the breastbone and two ribs were pulled apart. After about a minute and a half, his heart began to function again.

Walter spent four days unconscious and remained in the University Hospital as a patient until he was discharged ten days later.

On the day before he was discharged, Dr. Wyant visited Walter and gave him the fifty-dollar payment. Walter questioned whether this sum was worth it for all they had put him through. Dr. Wyant responded that fifty dollars was all they had bargained for, but he could give a larger sum for a complete release signed by Walter's mother or elder sister.

The doctors did conclude, as a result of the experiment, that Fluoromar had too narrow a margin of safety, and it was withdrawn from use in the University Hospital.

Walter Halushka sued the doctors on two grounds, trespass to the person and negligence. A jury trial followed and Walter was awarded 450 times the amount of the experiment fee — $22,500, a fair sum of money in the early 1960s. The defendant doctors and other named parties appealed to the Saskatchewan Court of Appeal.

The appeal court confirmed that Doctors Wyant and Merriman admitted that the cardiac arrest would not have occurred other than for the test. The court goes on: "The attachment of electrodes, the administration of anaesthetic and the insertion of the catheter were each an intentional application of force to the person . . . when taken as a whole they certainly constitute a trespass which would be actionable *unless done with consent.*"

Of course, one's initial response is — he signed the consent form. In ordinary medical practice, the consent given by a *patient* to a physician or surgeon, to be effective, must be "informed" consent freely given. It is the doctor's duty to give a fair and reasonable explanation of the proposed treatment, including the probable effects and any special or unusual risks.

Walter was not a patient, merely a student lab animal. What standard of information should he have expected? Justice Hall, speaking for the court: "In my opinion the duty imposed upon those engaged in medical research . . . to those who offer themselves as subject for experimentation . . . is *at least as great as, if not greater than,* the duty owed by the ordinary physician or surgeon to his patient."

Walter was entitled to a full and frank disclosure. He was not told the new drug was not known to the doctors, nor the risk involved with its use. It was, in light of the circumstances, *not* a "safe test."

He was not informed that the catheter would be advanced to and through his heart, but was led to believe it would only be inserted in the vein in his arm.

The court concluded this last fact might very well, if known to Walter, have discouraged him from consenting to the test. (It certainly would have discouraged us.)

The doctors' appeal was dismissed, with costs to be paid to Walter as well as the amount of the original judgment.

Unorthodox Therapy

In 1942, Ruth Clark was twenty years old, unmarried, and employed at a café in Melfort, Saskatchewan. According to the Criminal Code at that time, rape consisted in a man having carnal knowledge of a woman who was not his wife without her consent, or when consent had been extorted by threats or by fear of bodily harm or by impersonation of the woman's husband or by false and fraudulent representations as to the nature and quality of the act. Mr. Harms, the fittingly named accused, was a man of sixty-three years, who lived in Saskatoon, Saskatchewan, with his wife and family. In his own words, he travelled around from place to place and made his living massaging people.

In August of 1942, he was in Melfort. He had taken a room over the café where Ruth Clark worked. Ruth had been suffering from a pain in her chest and her father had advised to see Mr. Harms, who he knew as "Dr. Harms."

Mr. Harms took her to his room where she told him about the pain. He then assured her that he could correct the problem with a treatment which, though usually expensive, he would make free for her. He suggested that if she returned that night after her work, he would have the treatment ready for her.

Having finished her work about midnight, she returned, was admitted to his room, and had the door locked behind her. On the table was a tumbler containing some yellow liquid. Mr. Harms asked Ruth to drink it and, trustingly, she did so, asking him what it was. He replied that it was "just a couple of pills." He then suggested that she should lie down on his bed and "let the stuff settle." She said that it made her dizzy. After a while, he poured some liquid from another bottle into a glass and gave it to her to drink. She did so but said that it did not seem to have any immediate effect on her. After a further interval, he produced a match box from which he took two pills. Coming over to her, he told her that he was going to insert them in her "private parts." After removing her undergarments he made the insertion.

Meanwhile, unobserved by her, he had removed his own undergarment. He then got on top of her and attempted to excite her for the purpose of establishing sexual connection with her, saying all the while that he was doing it to make the pills operative. She objected and pushed him away, but he maintained that this action was necessary to produce an effective cure. After further futile efforts, he desisted, but he observed to her that if she insisted on being un-cooperative, she would have to take the consequences. Ultimately, she yielded, and he succeeded in having intercourse with her. She fell asleep and awoke some four hours later, Mr. Harms lay on the bed beside her. He told her that she had better go home and again expressed his confidence that she would be alright and would find her problem resolved.

About a month later, Mr. Harms was again in Melfort. As her physical complaints had not resolved, Ruth went to see him and accused him of "fooling her." He suggested that she should wait a little longer. She asked him for some more of the pills with which he had treated her. He gave her two, but instead of using them, she took them to a qualified physician under whose observation she then placed herself.

Two months later this physician declared her to be pregnant, and she subsequently gave birth.

Several days later, the police, who had been called upon to investigate this situation, obtained a statement from Mr. Harms. The pills were examined by a police expert and found to contain a contraceptive.

In a subsequent jury trial, Mr. Harms was convicted of rape and it is from this charge that he appealed. The position of his lawyer at this point was that Ruth must be held to have known the nature and quality of Mr. Harm's act since it was apparent to her. Mr. Harm's counsel goes on to submit that in the circumstances she gave an unqualified consent. The Appeal Court looked at the matter quite differently. While it may be conceded that Ruth knew the meaning of carnal knowledge as a sexual act, it was clear to the court that she was so well aware of the possible ill consequences that she would definitely be indisposed to run the risk for the sorry satisfaction of indulging in sexual intercourse with a man like the prisoner. She did it because she was led by false and fraudulent representations to believe that it was part of a treatment which would correct her physical disorder. In the opinion of the court, the jury was free to decide that the nature and quality of the act was pathological and not carnal. As the consent here was induced by false or fraudulent representations as to the nature and quality of the act, consent was obtained against her will.

The true law then was that consent or submission obtained by fraud was not a defence to a charge of rape. Thus, a man is deemed guilty of rape if he succeeds by fraud no less than by force in overcoming a woman's permanent will to virtue. The sentence was affirmed.

That's Gratitude for You

We have seen the complex nature of relationships between doctors and their patients. It becomes apparent that unsavoury and unprofessional behaviour will not be accepted. What then of a doctor who acts promptly, professionally, is well motivated throughout the management of a case, and carries on a competent, careful, and conscientious treatment strictly in accordance with the required standard of care as could be expected; who is, in fact, responsible for saving the life of a patient — who subsequently sues him?

Fifty-seven-year-old Mrs. Georgette Mallitt, in the early afternoon of June 30, 1979, was rushed unconscious by ambulance to the Kirkland and District Hospital in Kirkland Lake, Ontario. The car in which she had been a passenger, driven by her husband, had collided head-on with a truck. Sadly, her husband had been killed and she had suffered serious injuries.

On arrival at the hospital, she was attended by Dr. David Shulman, a family physician who served two or three shifts a week in the emergency department. Mrs. Mallitt had severe head and face injuries and was bleeding profusely. She appeared to be suffering from shock from blood loss, and the doctor ordered that she be given intravenous glucose followed immediately by Ringers' Lactate. The administration of a volume expander, such as Ringers' Lactate is standard medical procedure in cases of this nature. If the patient responds with sufficiently increased blood pressure, transfusions of blood are administered to carry essential oxygen to tissues, and remove waste products, and prevent damage to vital organs.

Right about now, a nurse discovered a card in Mrs. Mallitt's purse, identifying her as a Jehovah's Witness and requesting, on the basis of her religious convictions, that she be given no blood transfusions under any circumstances. The card was not dated or witnessed, but was printed in French and was signed by Mrs. Mallitt. The rejection of blood transfusions is based on the firm belief held by Jehovah's Witnesses, founded on their interpretation of the Scriptures, that the acceptance of blood will result in a forfeiture of their opportunity for resurrection and eternal salvation. Dr. Shulman was promptly advised of the card.

Mrs. Mallitt was next examined by a surgeon on duty in the hospital.

He concluded, as had Dr. Shulman, that to avoid irreversible shock it was vital to maintain Mrs. Mallitt's blood volume. He transferred Mrs. Mallitt to the X-ray department, however, before X-rays could be satisfactorily completed, her condition deteriorated. Her blood pressure dropped markedly, respiration became distressed, and her level of consciousness dropped as well. She continued to bleed profusely and was in critical condition.

Dr. Shulman concluded that transfusions were necessary to replace Mrs. Mallitt's blood loss and preserve her life. He personally administered transfusions to her in spite of the card. She was then transferred to the intensive care unit. Dr. Shulman was clearly aware of the religious objection to blood by his patient. He accepted full responsibility for the decision to administer the transfusions.

Approximately three hours later, Mrs. Mallitt's daughter, Céline Bission, arrived from Timmins, accompanied by her husband and a local church elder. She strongly objected to her mother having been given blood, notwithstanding Dr. Shulman's opinion as to the medical necessity of the transfusions, Mrs. Bission remained adamantly opposed to them and signed a document specifically prohibiting blood transfusions. Dr. Shulman did not follow her instructions. In his opinion, the blood transfusions were necessary to save Mrs. Mallitt's life.

By about midnight, the patient's condition had stabilized sufficiently for her to be transferred early the next day by air ambulance to hospital in Toronto where she received no further blood transfusions. In August, she was discharged and happily made a very good recovery from her injuries.

Approximately a year after the accident, Mrs. Mallitt brought an action against the doctor, the hospital, its executive directors, and four nurses, alleging that the administration of the blood transfusions in the circumstances of her case constituted both negligence and assault and battery and subjected her to religious discrimination. The matter was tried, and Mr. Justice Donnelly dismissed the action against all the defendants except Dr. Shulman. The judge concluded that Mrs. Mallitt's card validly restricted Dr. Shulman's right to treat the patient, and that the administration of blood constituted a battery on the patient. Mrs. Mallitt was awarded $20,000 in damages, but there was no award as to costs. Dr. Shulman appealed, Mrs. Mallitt cross-appealed, taking the matter to the Ontario Court of Appeal.

As found by the trial judge, the court determined that there was no negligence on the doctor's part; that he had acted promptly,

professionally, was well motivated and competent. Both the trial judge and Court of Appeal determined that the doctor's treatment of Mrs. Mallitt may well have been responsible for saving her life. What then was the legal effect of the card and was the doctor bound to honour its instructions? The situation, of course, was one of emergency, and conscious instructions could not be obtained.

Any intentional, nonconsensual touching which is harmful or offensive to a person's reasonable sense of dignity can be the subject of a court action. There are no special exceptions for medical care other than in emergency situations. Therefore, patients have a very decisive role in the medical decision-making process. In our legal system, informed consent is a means of protecting a patient's right to control his or her medical treatment. No medical procedure may be undertaken without the patient's consent obtained after the patient has been provided with enough information to evaluate the risks and benefits of the proposed treatment and other available options. The right of self-determination also includes the right to refuse medical treatment. The emergency situation that Mrs. Mallitt found herself in is an exception to this general rule requiring a patient's prior consent. Where immediate attention is necessary to save life or preserve the health of a person who by reason of unconsciousness or extreme illness is not capable of giving or withholding consent, a doctor can proceed without the patient's consent. It is clear that Dr. Shulman faced an emergency. He had an unconscious, critically ill patient on his hands; one who, in his opinion, needed blood transfusions to save her life. The law however does not prohibit a patient from withholding a consent to emergency medical treatment nor does the law prevent a doctor from following his patient's instructions.

The distinguishing feature in this case, of course, is the Jehovah's Witness card on the person of the unconscious patient. It cannot be a meaningless piece of paper. In the circumstances, the instructions on the card imposed a valid restriction on the emergency treatment that could be provided to Mrs. Mallitt and prevented blood transfusions. This was the only way possible to notify doctors or other providers of health care should Mrs. Mallitt be unconscious or otherwise unable to convey her wish to not receive blood transfusions. There is no suggestion that she wished to die. Her rejection of blood transfusions was based on her firm religious belief. It is not then for the doctor to second guess the reasonableness of the decision nor to pass judgment on the religious principles which motivated this decision.

Mrs. Mallitt's daughter's instructions merely confirmed her mother's wishes. The problem, of course, facing a doctor, is that on the one hand, if he administers blood in the situation and saves the patient's life, the patient can hold him responsible for battery. On the other hand, if the doctor follows the patient's instructions and as a consequence the patient dies, the doctor might face an action by the patient's relatives and dependents alleging that notwithstanding the card, the deceased would, if conscious, have accepted blood in the face of imminent death, and the doctor was negligent in failing to administer the transfusions.

This latter point was raised by Dr. Shulman's lawyers and the court stated that the second result is not permissible. The doctor cannot be held to have violated his legal duty or professional responsibility toward the patient or the patient's relatives and dependents when he honours the Jehovah's Witness card and respects the patient's right to control her body in accordance with the dictates of her conscience.

When members of a faith choose to carry cards intended to notify doctors and other providers of health care that they reject certain types of medical treatment, they must accept the consequences of their decision. If harmful consequences follow, the responsibility is entirely theirs, not the doctor's. In the argument about the amount of money that was awarded as damages, the court held that $20,000 was not beyond the range of damages appropriate to an interference of this nature.

The best intentions of a doctor then have to be tempered by the fact that the patient has absolute control over his or her own body.

LANDOWNERS

The Landlord Was Jealous

Pam Freedman, a college student, lived in an apartment building. She moaned so loudly whilst enjoying intimate relations that neighbouring children were awakened. Ms. Philion, who previously had lived in the flat below Ms. Freedman, claimed that while she had had no problem with the previous tenant, once Ms. Freedman and her boyfriend Mike Papadimos moved in, the moaning was so loud that she and other tenants were greatly (and understandably) disturbed. Ms. Philion complained too about the frequency of this amorous cacaphony. Several nights a week, she indicated, and sometimes two or three times an evening, she was alerted to activity by her neighbours. She indicated that the duration of moaning could be anywhere between thirty and sixty minutes. Her children were awakened on many occasions, and the family eventually had to vacate their apartment because of the sexual sighing. Mr. and Mrs. Abott, who lived above Ms. Freedman's flat also said that they were disturbed by what some have referred to as "the urge to merge." The building superintendent too was awakened by the ululations of the amorous symphony. He pointed out that even when he went outside the building, he could still hear the moaning.

At trial, Ms. Freedman testified (probably to Mike Papadimos's chagrin) that Mike was only an occasional visitor, and, while acknowledging that she invited other boyfriends back to her apartment, she denied the frequency alleged by the other tenants.

She pointed out that the problem had less to do with the actual sounds emanating from the apartment than with the lack of proper insulation.

Her evidence showed that sounds of all the usual daily activities could easily be heard throughout all the apartments, disturbing the other tenants.

District Court Judge S. H. Murphy copiously referred to the provisions of the Ontario Landlord and Tenant Act in an attempt to ascertain whether or not the conduct complained of substantially interfered with the reasonable enjoyment of the premises for the usual purposes of the tenants and landlord. Carefully pointing out that there was no law against lovemaking, he went on to determine that where such activity creates sound in the extreme, the residential provisions of the legislation kick in. In a judicial determination of fact, he accepted the evidence of the other tenants and found that the conduct of Ms. Freeman substantially interfered with the reasonable enjoyment of the premises by the landlord and other tenants. He ordered the termination of the lease. Ms. Freeman, we understand, has since left for less intrusive and more receptive neighbours.

Landlord Raises the Roof

Mr. Jones rented a cottage from Lady Emily Foley. When the term of his tenancy expired, he decided that he would stay on, notwithstanding the end of the arrangement, and he wrongfully refused to give up possession. Lady Emily wanted possession of the cottage so she could pull it down and put up a brand new one to live in herself. She applied for and obtained a Justices' Warrant directing the constables to give her possession of the cottage after the expiration of twenty-one days from the date of the warrant.

However, Lady Emily, being a tad impatient, had her workmen remove the roof of the house later the same day she had obtained the Justices' Warrant. This she felt, would make it clear to Mr. Jones just what her intentions were. Alas, certain tiles and pieces of mortar unavoidably fell into the bedroom, damaging Mr. Jones's furniture.

Lady Emily was sued by Mr. Jones for trespass and, more importantly, injury to his furniture. In the jury's opinion, her removal of the roof amounted to forceable entry, and Lady Emily was held to be responsible for any damages that Mr. Jones or his furniture suffered.

Lady Emily appealed. Mr. Justice Day held the opinion that Mr. Jones had no cause of action. He further found that Mr. Jones's refusal to leave after Lady Emily had obtained an Order for Possession, was very "embarrassing for her." The effect of the warrant that she obtained from the justices, though its execution was delayed for twenty-one days, did not require her to wait to avail herself of the warrant. Lady Emily, in the court's opinion, notwithstanding that portions of the roof fell into the bedroom and caused damage to Mr. Jones' personal goods, was perfectly justified in doing what she did. Any injury that happened to Mr. Jones's furniture was not due to any unlawful act on her part but was the result of his own obstinacy in unlawfully insisting on remaining where he was. The court felt that he must put up with the consequences. Lady Emily did not purposely damage the goods. The removal of the roof was effected not with the object of injuring Mr. Jones or his goods but simply as a step in the demolition of Lady Emily's own house. Mr. Justice Day went on to state that:

> I am clearly of the opinion that what was done here did not amount to a forceable entry. It does not belong to the class of acts at which the statutes of forceable entry are aimed. The Plaintiff has established no cause of action. Judgment must be entered for the Defendant.

If ripping the roof off a house that someone is occupying is not a forceable entry, we are left to ponder what would be.

You Pays Your Taxes and Takes Your Chances

Goods and services tax, income tax, realty tax, retail sales tax: you name it, we pay it. Are we really right up there with the most over-taxed generations? What if you pay your realty tax but the city doesn't believe that you did? Dennis Hunt found out what if the hard way.

Hunt owned land in Renfrew County in Ontario. He had occupied the property for several years. Mistakenly, the municipal authorities believed that Michael McNulty, Sr. owned the land. In fact, Michael McNulty, Sr., owned the adjacent property. Hunt paid his taxes, McNulty did not. The municipality sold McNulty's lands because of his default — and included Dennis Hunt's property in the sale. The property sold again and the municipality sent a notice of the sale to Hunt, who claimed that he never received it.

Dennis Hunt died, and his wife sought to have the land returned to her. The court decided that the tax sales legislation gave the person who bought the property from the municipality a good and valid title that could not be challenged or set aside. The law therefore took away all of Hunt's rights in the property and extinguished his beneficiaries' rights.

The Tax Sales Law provided the new owner and later purchasers with valid title. Thus, Hunt, who paid his realty taxes and did nothing improper, lost his property and his beneficiary, his wife, lost her interest in the land.

Can she do anything about it? Yes. She can sue the municipality for negligence, though, as the court points out, there may be other obstacles to overcome. Amazing. You pay your taxes, agreeable or not, you do nothing wrong, yet you end up losing your land and are now in a lawsuit, at your expense, against an economically stronger party. It's something to think about when your next realty tax assessment notice arrives.

THE FUN NEW QUIZ CARD! THE BIGGEST PRIZES!

Super Scratch — WIN A CRUISE!

You could soon be sailing the clear blue waters of the Caribbean on a fantastic two week luxury cruise for two! First decide whether the statement below is true or false. If you pick the right answer, uncover the panel underneath to reveal a number. If it matches the winning number on the claims hotline, you've won a Caribbean cruise!!

PLAY NOW!

A BLACK WIDOW IS A TYPE OF WASP

TRUE ☐ FALSE ✓

118181

Scratch & Match!

If you pick the correct answer rub off all three panels to reveal three letters. If you uncover TWO matching letters you've won a prize! Check out the claims hotline to find out which prize you can claim with the matching letters you have uncovered!

See over for claim details.

A TARANTULA IS A TYPE OF BEETLE

TRUE ☐ FALSE ✓

M M O

PRIZES!
★ One of 3 SONY 27" STEREO TVs!
★ One of 2 SONY CAMCORDERS!
★ THE TOP 50 MUSIC CDs!
★ One of 2 JVS HI-FIS!
★ One of 4 NINTENDO SYSTEMS PLUS 10 GAMES!!
★ One of 2 WEEKENDS IN NEW YORK!
★ One of 5 $500 CASH PRIZES!
★ A $1000 MOUNTAINBIKE
★ FANTASTIC JEWELRY RUNNER-UP GIFTS!

Ticket to Fly!

This is your chance to fly worldwide with the Superscratch! First decide whether the statement below is true or false. If you pick it right scratch the three panels above. If you uncover THREE matching symbols check the winner's panel to see what you've won!

BOMBAY IS IN PAKISTAN

TRUE ☐ FALSE ✓

A A A A TRIP TO PARIS!
☀ A HOLIDAY IN FLORIDA!
☀ HOLIDAY IN BARBADOS!
✿✿✿ [2 ADULTS, TWO KIDS]

WIN THIS CAR! WORTH $30,000!

502163

First decide whether the statement below is true or false. If you pick the right answer, rub off the panel on the car to reveal a number. If that number exactly matches the winning number on the hotline, this fantastic 1995 Toyota Previa LE worth $30,000 is all yours!!

AN OSTRICH CANNOT FLY

TRUE ✓ FALSE ☐

SUPER CASH GRAB!
FIVE $5,000 PRIZES TO WIN!

58448

Here's where you could grab $5,000 in cash prizes! First decide whether below's statement is true or false. Then scratch off all of these numbers. If the winning number in the hotline is among these numbers you win $5,000!!

HAWAII IS IN THE INDIAN OCEAN

TRUE ☐ FALSE ✓

The Moths of Hope

Early in December of 1956, Mr. and Mrs. Scott-Polson, having heard that Mr. Hope's home on Wesley Drive in Saanich, British Columbia, was for sale, inspected it two or three times in a fairly casual manner. They finally decided to buy the house, and the actual agreement was signed several days later.

Mr. Scott-Polson later stated that when he asked Mr. Hope about the insulation in the house, he was told that the house was "well insulated." Mr. Hope, however, denied that he had used this expression, but had said that the house was "fully insulated." As you may be aware, insulation has become a serious issue over the last fifteen years. In fact, there isn't an Agreement of Purchase and Sale that doesn't concern itself with whether or not the insulation contains urea formaldehyde foam. It is not usual today to find any agreement without at least a condition or warranty to protect an unsuspecting buyer.

When Mr. and Mrs. Scott-Polson inspected Mr. Hope's house, they did not notice any signs of problems nor did they talk about them. However, after taking possession of the house, they discovered that the insulation in the walls might be inadequate; they could not get the temperature in the house above fifty-nine degrees. They hired a heating contractor to alter the ducts of the hot air system. In the course of his work, he opened up a wall of the house. After the alterations, the Scott-Polsons were able to maintain a temperature of seventy degrees in the house.

Some two weeks later, large quantities of moths and grubs appeared in every room of the house, in the cupboards and in drawers. The infestation was particularly evident near the wall that had been opened by the heating contractor. The Scott-Polsons were forced to vacate the house and a pest-control expert was summoned. He found that the insulation in the house was infested with common clothes moths.

An entomologist was called in and took samples of the insulation. He found moth life in all its stages, and said that it could have taken up to two years to achieve an infestation such as this. The insulation material in the house contained wool and horse hair: a perfect breeding ground for the moths. Furthermore, it seems that the ideal temperature for moth propagation lay between seventy-five and eighty degrees. At this temperature the life cycle of the moth was approximately fifty to ninety days. At cooler temperatures, the life cycle could be extended to as long as two and a half years. He said that the moths could complete their whole life cycle in the insulation between the walls of the house, with a few possibly escaping underneath the moulding where the wall joined the concrete floor. Infestation would not necessarily be apparent to an occupant of the house if the walls were not opened up.

The Scott-Polsons sued for their money back and damages. The vendor, Mr. Hope, testified that at the time he sold the house, he did not know that there was a problem. He also confirmed that he kept the temperature of the house under sixty degrees. A neighbour who appeared as a witness stated that he had seen the defendant sitting in the house reading near the window, and that he had seen large numbers of small moths near the reading lamp. However, his place of observation was at least thirty or forty feet from the place where the defendant was sitting inside the house and he could not possibly know whether the moths he saw were inside or outside the house.

The court reached the conclusion that the defendant was not aware of the moth infestation at the time he sold the house. In a case of this type — a "latent defect" of quality — the Scott-Polsons would have to prove either breach of warranty or fraud to be entitled to a remedy. In this case, no fraud existed: Mr. Hope did not know of the infestation. The statement that was made about the insulation really related to the ability of the insulation to prevent the passage of heat or cold. This was understood by the Scott-Polsons. Mr. Justice McLean found that the law was clear that there was no implied warranty that a residential property be fit for human habitation. This leaves us to ponder what, exactly, a residential property *should* be fit for. He held that there was no warranty, either express or implied and no fraud committed. As a consequence, the only happy party here is the entomologist. The Scott-Polsons, who hoped to succeed, were moth-balled.

Lawyer Makes the Earth Move

What makes this case fairly bizarre is its subject matter: a house — the exact same house — which was situated on each of two parcels of land at the time that each of the two lenders advanced their loans to the same borrowers. In 1987 a lawyer, Faulkner by name, took out a mortgage from the Toronto Dominion Bank on a property that he owned in the Township of Goulbourn in the Province of Ontario for the sum of $50,000. At the time that the bank agreed to mortgage the property, a house stood on it. The normal procedure was followed, and the mortgage was duly registered in the local land registry office.

Several years went by, and, without the bank's knowledge, Faulkner had the house moved from the first property in Goulbourn to lands owned by his spouse in the township of West Carleton. The following year, his spouse conveyed the second property in West Carleton to herself and Faulkner, who then held title to it. At about the same time, he and his wife arranged for a mortgage of the second property with Crown Trust for the sum of $55,080. At the time the Crown Trust mortgage was given, the house stood on the second property. The record showed that there was no registration on the title to the property in West Carleton of any mortgage or claim by the Toronto Dominion Bank in relation to the house. Again following the proper conveyancing procedures, Crown Trust had its mortgage duly registered in the local land registry office for the Township of West Carleton. Both the Toronto Dominion Bank and Crown Trust advanced the full funds on their respective mortgages.

The trial judges' finding of fact determined that Faulkner had wrongfully removed the house from the first property to the second property, and that Crown Trust, the second mortgagors, had not been given any notice that the house had been moved, nor any notice of the Toronto Dominion Bank's claim, until quite a bit of time after it had already fully funded the mortgage. However, the trial judge did find that the Toronto Dominion Bank had a priority interest. He held that Faulkner was liable in damages to the bank for the value of the house, and that the bank was also entitled to an order for a lien upon the house at its location on the second property unless there was a misconduct or omission on the part of the Toronto Dominion Bank which would disentitle it. Having found that there was no misconduct or omission, and the bank could not have easily determined that the house had been moved from the first property, the bank's priority was fixed.

It is from this decision that Crown Trust appealed. Mr. Justice Katzman delivered the Appeal Court decision. He allowed the appeal and determined that an order should be issued declaring that the Crown Trust mortgage had priority over the Toronto Dominion Bank's interest in both the second property in the township of West Carleton and in the house that now sat on it. The court decided that where equities are equal, the legal title would prevail; if two claims were equally meritorious, there was really no ground, in the court's opinion, for depriving Crown Trust, who had the legal estate, of the priority which its estate conferred.

The Toronto Dominion Bank's claim to a lien on the house, or to the land to which is was removed, must yield to the mortgage on the second property. Though the trial judge did correctly conclude that the Toronto Dominion Bank was entitled to damages from the defendant, who wrongfully removed the house, the question of priorities finding in favour of the bank was not the position of this court. The court does however point out that Faulkner, a lawyer, has since been disbarred.

Cemetery Evicts Its Tenants

The commercial ingenuity abounding in our society is truly amazing. There has been recently a spate of advertising for do-it-yourself coffins. The advertiser will supply the plans and you and your family can build final homes for your loved ones. It's said to be an aid to grieving. Our society is profoundly interested in death, dying and the afterlife. Woody Allen has pointed out on more than one occasion that he does not believe that there is life after death, but just in case he is going to bring a change of underwear.

The Methodist Episcopal Church in the City of Pittsburgh purchased a piece of ground to use as a graveyard, and this is how it was dedicated and used. Over time, the property was transferred to the Centenary Board of the Pittsburgh Conference of the Methodist Episcopal Church. As the city grew, the area around the cemetery became heavily built up. The grounds ceased to be used any longer for interments, in fact, many bodies were removed by relatives to other cemeteries. Consequently, the cemetery wasn't bringing in enough money for the church to keep it in the proper order. The grounds became neglected and untidy.

The families who buried their loved ones here over the years presumably chose their final resting places carefully. Undoubtedly, they hoped that that they would remain appropriately undisturbed and surrounded by well-kept grounds and a peaceful atmosphere. This was not to be. An Act was passed entitled "An Act for the vacation and sale of the methodist burial-ground in the City of Pittsburgh and for removing the bodies therefrom."

This Act said that "from and after the passage of the Act it will be unlawful to make interments in the said burial ground; and after the removal of the bodies therein as provided for in the Act, the same will be vacated for burial purposes." It went on to authorize the "landlords" to purchase one or more suitable lots in some of the other cemeteries in the city and to remove to those lots all the remaining "residents" in the burial ground, where they were to be once again decently interred. The monuments and tombstones in the old burial ground were to be removed and set up over these new resting places. Once the eviction was complete, the commissioners were to sell the property in such a manner as they determined would be most advisable and most likely to realize the greatest income.

Interestingly, the proceeds from this sale were to be distributed first to pay the expense of the relocation and secondly to compensate the lot-

holders: one wonders when the cheques to the lot-holders might be cashed. The balance of the funds would then go to the congregation of the Methodist Episcopal Church. Not unexpectedly, relatives put forward objections on behalf of the dearly departed. The issue came down to whether or not the Act was constitutional.

At trial, the opinion of the court was that this was an unconstitutional infringement upon the lot-holders' rights. The Appeal Court held that the original grants were mere licences, what one might call "privilege to be buried in the lot described" exclusive of anybody else as long as this particular ground remained "the burying-ground of the church." These "tenants" had no title to the soil and would be required to vacate the ground should the place not continue to be used in this fashion. The court went on to make an interesting comparison to the grant of a pew in a church. In their opinion this gave the same kind of rights as those given by purchase of a burial plot in a graveyard. I'm not sure that the

analysis is fair: how many people are dying to get into church? The right of a pew was described as a "limited usufruct right" only. If the church became dilapidated or was destroyed by fire, the right of the pew owner was also destroyed.

The court followed this line of reasoning and decided that, indeed, the legislature was authorized to remove anything they deemed to be a nuisance, in this case the "tenants," from any ground used as a burying ground. Finally, the court was at pains to point out that entirely decomposed "tenants," those consisting only of bones, may not confer the same urgency to relocate as those that are recently interred. Giving proper lip service to the strong desire of family and friends that their departed ancestors not be disturbed, the court concluded that these feelings must yield to the higher consideration of the public good.

This seems to give new meaning to the words *final resting place*, doesn't it?

TRAVEL

Unchained Melody

A cruise. Doesn't that conjure up images of the loveboat? Having planned a vacation on the rolling waves one would pack the Gravol and expect to have a rollicking good time.

But your ship might have been commanded by Captain Franklin, the captain of the *Undaunted*.

The plaintiff, a Mr. P., was a passenger on the *Undaunted*. Everything was going swimmingly well on the cruise until a quarrel arose between Captain Franklin and some passengers, including Mr. P., regarding card-playing in a particular part of the vessel.

It appears that during the dispute Mr. P. said to the captain, in a quite insulting fashion, that the "ship was a floating hotel and the captain only the landlord." The captain quite obviously was seriously insulted by this apparently innocuous comment, and he ordered Mr. P. to be thrown into leg irons. This, in his opinion, was perfectly reasonable as there was no cabin available to lock Mr. P. in.

The voyage ended, Mr. P. was released, and he immediately sued Captain Franklin for false imprisonment. Mr. Justice Watson, in summing up the case, found that the captain had absolute control over the passengers and crew. The contract with the passenger, he said, was to carry, board, and lodge him, and the passenger had to obey all of the captain's reasonable orders. In fact, in an emergency, passengers might even have to act as crew on the ship. In cases of a passenger's misconduct, the captain was entitled to remove him or even imprison him for a short period, if necessary for the enforcement of the captain's lawful commands.

The rule of law as stated by the court was quite simple; the power of the captain is limited to the necessity of each individual case.

Captain Franklin stated at his trial that "he had reasonable and probable cause to believe, and honestly did believe, that a mutiny was imminent." Anybody can understand that. Certainly you've seen bridge games where the players behaved mutinously, haven't you? I once met a cribbage player who I was sure could easily inspire insurrection and insurgency.

Fortunately for Mr. P., the captain was required to prove the whole of his allegation. It would not, in the court's opinion, be sufficient that he did believe mutiny imminent; there would have to be reasonable cause for apprehending a mutiny. Captain Franklin appears merely to have been insulted by the epithet *landlord* hurled at him by Mr. P. Imprisoning the passenger under such circumstances would not be reasonable or justified, even though the word *landlord* was not altogether incorrect. The possibility of imprisonment for calling the captain names certainly would not encourage anyone to sail on the *Undaunted*.

If you ever have the urge to be thrown into leg irons, this ship might be the logical choice. Certainly, Captain Franklin is more akin to Captain Bly than to Captain Stubbing. Welcome to the Love Boat!

Passengers Walk the Plank

An American ship, the *William Brown*, left Liverpool bound for Philadelphia. Besides a heavy cargo, she was carrying a crew of seventeen and sixty-five passengers. About 250 miles southeast of Cape Race, Newfoundland, the vessel struck an iceberg and began to fill so rapidly with water that it became apparent that she would soon go down. A longboat and a jolly-boat were lowered into the water. The captain, second mate, seven crew members, and one passenger all got into the jolly-boat. The first mate, eight seamen (the remainder of the crew) and thirty-two passengers got into the longboat. This meant that forty-one people were crammed into a boat twenty-two and a half feet long, six feet in the beam and about three feet deep. Horrendously, the remaining thirty-one passengers were obliged to remain on board the ship, which went down approximately one and a half hours after striking the iceberg.

The following morning the jolly-boat and the longboat parted company. The captain gave the crew of the longboat directions and counsel before parting with them. He advised them to obey all the orders of the first mate as if they were his orders. The crew faithfully promised that they would do so.

Though the longboat was believed to be in good condition, she had not been in the water since leaving Liverpool, and as soon as she was launched she began to leak. She continued to leak the whole time, but the passengers had buckets and tins and managed to bale out enough water to make her hold her own. The jolly-boat was picked up with all hands by a French fishing lugger after having been out to sea six days. The evidence of these individuals at the trial later showed that when the two boats separated, the longboat and all aboard were, in their opinion, in great jeopardy. Even without a leak, she would not have supported one half her company, and had there been a "moderate blow she would have swamped very quickly." The poor survivors were half-naked and were crowded together like sheep in a pen.

So how did the longboat fare? The first mate told the captain that the longboat was unmanageable and that unless the captain would take some of the longboat's passengers into the jolly-boat, it would be necessary to cast lots and throw some overboard. The captain replied that he knew what would have to be done, but advised that it should be done only as a last resort.

Loaded as she was, the longboat survived throughout the night and another twenty-four hours before disaster struck. On the second morning, it began to rain. It continued to rain throughout that day and all night. The sea grew heavier, and the waves splashed over the boat's bow soaking all its occupants.

The crew now began to throw some of the passengers overboard. They did not stop until they had thrown over fourteen male passengers. Except for two married men and a small boy, these were all the male passengers still alive. Not one crew member was cast over.

Not one remark appears to have been made regarding what was being done or the necessity for doing it. The first mate did direct the crew not to part man and wife and not to throw over any women, otherwise there was no principle of selection. No lots were cast nor were the passengers consulted or informed about what was being done.

A crew member named Holmes was one of those most instrumental in throwing the passengers over. When a passenger named Askin was put out, he had struggled violently, and yet the boat had not sunk. Two men, very stiff with cold, who had somehow hidden themselves, were thrown over after daylight the next morning. Clearly there was no necessity for this as that same morning the weather cleared. The longboat was picked up that day by the ship *Crescent*.

Holmes was indicted under an Act which ordains that if any seaman shall commit manslaughter upon the high seas, on conviction he shall be imprisoned and fined. The indictment charged that Holmes, with force and unlawfully and feloniously "did assault and cast and throw Askin from the vessel into the high seas by means of which Askin in and with the waters was suffocated and drowned."

The evidence at trial indicated that Holmes was a man of character. He had been the last of the crew to leave the sinking ship. His efforts to save the passengers at the time the ship struck had been conspicuous. He was kind and obliging in every respect both to passengers and to his ship-mates. In the longboat he had given all his clothes except his shirt and pantaloons to the women to try and keep them warm.

Holmes's defence was that the homicide was necessary to self-preservation. The prosecution's position was that since the danger was not of the sort that was instant, overwhelming, and left no choice of means or moment for deliberation, Holmes was guilty. He had no right to sacrifice the lives of sixteen fellow beings. Peril, even extreme peril, was not enough to justify this action. The law did not give seamen the power to jettison human beings as if they were cargo; to throw overboard for their own safety whoever they may choose.

The prosecutor indicated that it is because a sailor is expected to expose himself to every danger that by every law his wages are secure to him. The seamen's claims are a "sacred lien," and "if only a single nail of the ship is left, they are entitled to it." Exposure, risk, hardship, and death are the sailor's vocation; the seamen's daily bread.

The position for the defence was substantially different, as one might expect. In fact, there was a suggestion that the case should be tried in a longboat sunk to its gunwales and carrying forty-one half-naked starved, and shivering wretches; leaking from below and filling from above; One hundred leagues from land in the dead of night and surrounded by ice; unmanageable and subject to near-certain destruction from the most changeful of the elements — the winds and the waves.

Mr. Justice Baldwin impressed strongly upon the jury that the mere absence of malice did not render homicide excusable. In cases such as these, the law neither excuses the act nor permits it to be justified as innocent. It is the law of necessity alone which can disarm the vindicatory justice of the country. The court went on to state that where a case does arise which embraces the law of necessity, then the penal laws pass over such a case in silence, for the law is made to meet only the ordinary exigencies of life. A case does not become one of necessity unless all ordinary means of self-preservation have been exhausted. The peril must be instant, overwhelming and must leave no alternative to losing one's own life other than to take the life of another person.

When transportation is hired, the owners of a vehicle are bound to transport the passengers to their destination if a fare is accepted. Any defect in the vehicle, any lack of care or skill, any injuries done to passengers and employees, the owner is liable for. The passenger's position is different from that of the officers and seamen; it is the sailor who must encounter the hardships and perils of the voyage, and this does not change when the ship is lost at sea and all aboard have taken to the lifeboats for safety. Danger does not absolve the sailor from his duty, he is bound as before to undergo whatever hazard is necessary to preserve the boat and the passengers. He certainly has no right to sacrifice the passengers for his own safety. The court did admit that sailor and sailor can lawfully struggle with each other for the plank which can save but one, but if a passenger is on the plank even "the law of necessity" does not justify the sailor who takes it from the passenger.

In this case, one of unusual hardship, the court also looked at the method of selection for survival. It was decided that there should have been consultation over the choice of who was to survive and who was to die so that all on the boat could have had an equal chance for life. What this mode of selection should have been is a question that is not without major difficulty.

When a ship is no danger of sinking but sustenance is exhausted and a sacrifice of one person is necessary to allow the survival of the others, selection is generally agreed to be by lot. This, it appears, was the path suggested by the captain to the first mate.

The jury took sixteen hours to return with their verdict. Holmes was

Look Before You Leap

There are forms of transportation other than marine that can be detrimental to one's health. It seems that one is not even safe strolling a designated pedestrian path — the city sidewalk.

A chauffeur in the employ of Peerless Transportation Company in New York City found himself in a drama that started in an alley near 26th Street and Third Avenue in Manhattan. An unnamed man was relieved of his portable goods by two nondescript highwaymen in this alley. They pressed their point with the use of a fairly persuasive pistol. Laden with their loot, but not impeded, they abruptly departed. The victim gave chase down 26th Street towards Second Avenue, where the highwaymen separated. The pursuer's ardour was unabated, and he focused on the capture of the man with the pistol.

This ruffian boarded a taxicab driven by the chauffeur who worked for Peerless Transportation Company. The cab quickly veered south on Second Avenue towards 25th Street. The driver's story was that his uninvited guest had advised him to move at once after boarding the cab, and had added finality to this command by the appropriate gesture with the pistol addressed to the driver's sacroiliac.

The chauffeur had proceeded fairly reluctantly for about fifteen feet when he beheld the victim, now accompanied by a cohort of law-abiding citizens, running after him screeching, "Stop, thief!" The pursuing posse gained on the cab and its contents, and the holdup man, sensing a certain insecurity, advised the driver that if there was the slightest lapse in obedience to his commands, then the chauffeur would suffer the loss of his brains.

This prospect was so horrible to the humble chauffeur, and his apprehension was so great, and the pursuers so maddening that he quickly threw his vehicle out of first gear, pulled on the emergency brake, jammed on the regular brakes, and, although the motor was still running, swung open the door to his left and jumped out of the car.

Thus abandoning his car and passenger, the chauffeur ran towards 26th Street . . . and then turned to look. He saw his cab proceeding south towards 24th Street. He saw it mount the sidewalk. He saw that it was now not only driverless but passengerless, and he saw it hit and injure (comparatively slightly, thank goodness) Mrs. Mary Cordas and her two infant children. Mary Cordas, on behalf of herself, her children, and Mr. Cordas, sued the defendant for damages, basing their action on the negligence of the chauffeur in abandoning his cab. The hold-up man was later apprehended in the cellar of a local hospital where he been followed by several of the posse.

Mr. Justice Carlin of the City Court of New York, in a judgment peppered with references to Shakespeare, indicated that the test of actionable negligence was based on what reasonably prudent men would have done in the same circumstances. He recognized that the driver's love of his own security took his reason prisoner. The attorney acting on behalf of the plaintiffs conceded to the court that the driver had faced an emergency, but felt that the public at large should be immune to injury by dangerous instruments such as cars, even when the driver was under the belief that his life was in danger. Drivers cannot be permitted to abandon vehicles which then injure third parties.

The court recognized that there are people in society who "bridge the yawning chasm with a leap, [who] outstare the sternest eyes, outbrave the heart most daring on the earth, pluck young sucking cubs from the she-bear and mock the lion when he roars for prey." These people are

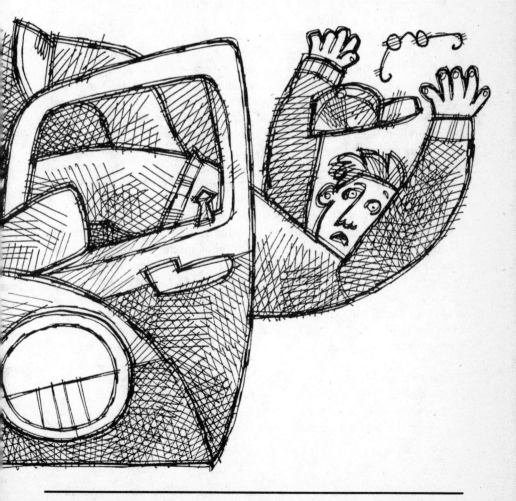

made of sterner stuff that the ordinary man, upon whom the law places no duty of emulation. If an individual is placed in sudden peril from which death might ensue, the law does not impel another to rescue that party nor does it condemn that party for failure to rescue. The court went on to say that the law in the State of New York does not hold one in an emergency to the exercise of that mature judgment required of him or her under circumstances where he or she has an opportunity for deliberate action.

The chauffeur — an ordinary man — acted instantaneously during a most harrowing experience. To call him negligent would be to brand him a coward; the court did not do so, no matter what swaggering heros "whose valour plucks dead lions by the beard" may have felt. The court was loathe to see the plaintiffs go without recovery, though their damages were slight, but was unable to hold the defendant driver liable.

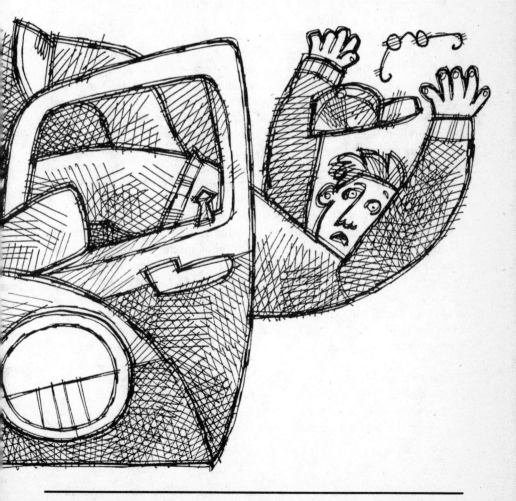

Dining and Whining

Mr. Bahner is young, personable, and intelligent. His father was the leader of a political party in his homeland, and hè had assisted his father in elections and other political activities. He had qualified in his own country as a commercial pilot and had a Canadian licence to operate single-engine commercial aircraft.

One fine August evening, Mr. Bahner took two friends, Mr. and Mrs. Duncan, to dinner at Trader Vic's, a restaurant operated by the defendant, Marwest Hotel Co. Ltd., at the Bayshore Inn in Vancouver. Trader Vic's was generally regarded as a superior sort of eating place. The three started their dinner at the continental hour of about 10:30 P.M. Mr. Bahner, as host, ordered a bottle of wine, a respectable French wine, to accompany dinner. No other drinks were served.

There was clear evidence that this was an entirely sober and decorous party, and that Mr. Bahner had drunk only three or four small glasses of wine with his meal. At no time was he in any way even slightly tipsy. By about 11:30 P.M., the party had consumed most of their dinner and about half their bottle of wine. Their waiter, James Gee, asked Mr. Bahner if he would like another bottle, and he said that he would. Five minutes later, a bottle was brought to them, already open, and left in the wine cooler.

The first bottle of wine had been finished by 11:50 P.M., but the second bottle had not been touched. At this time the waiter, James Gee, came to the table to advise Mr. Bahner that he must, as provided by provincial law consume the entire contents of the second bottle of wine before midnight. After that hour in British Columbia, it was illegal to drink wine in a restaurant. Doesn't this situation remind you of Cinderella?

Mr. Bahner said that the bottle of wine couldn't possibly be drunk within the next ten minutes without everyone getting drunk. The waiter agreed but said that they would have to pay for the wine anyway. Mr. Bahner refused to do so. The manager, Harvey Chen, was summoned. Harvey Chen insisted that since Mr. Bahner had ordered the wine, he must pay for it. Mr. Bahner, saying that he had not been told about the time limits, refused to pay for it unless he could take it with him. Mr. Chen advised him that, also under provincial law, he could not take the wine.

One can easily imagine the effect upon a person accustomed to more tolerant customs of a demand to pay for a bottle of wine which one can neither drink nor carry away. Even though there might be civil liability in these circumstances, it is impossible, by any stretch of imagination, to

conceive that Mr. Bahner was guilty of any criminal act.

Into this unfortunate situation now enters Rocky, the Pinkerton Detective Agency's security guard. This agency was engaged by the hotel company to provide security services for the hotel. Rocky was summoned by the manager. Rocky insisted that Mr. Bahner had to pay for the wine or the police would be called.

At this point Mr. Bahner paid his dinner bill — some $50 or $60 and tipped the waiter, an extraordinarily magnanimous gesture under the circumstances, but he did not pay for the second bottle of wine. He and his guests then got up from the table and started to leave the hotel. He found the exit blocked by Rocky, who intimidatingly indicated to him that he could not leave and that the police were going to be called in.

Mr. Bahner behaved with admirable restraint. He made no attempt to force his way past Rocky the security guard, nor did he go to any other exits. He just waited.

Soon, two uniformed policemen arrived. One, Constable Muir, became a defendant in this court application. Muir told Mr. Bahner that if he did not pay for the wine he would be arrested. Mr. Bahner responded by asking Constable Muir whether he might be able to go to his car to get a toothbrush before he was taken away. Constable Muir put him under arrest for refusing to pay for the wine.

The patrol wagon was called, Mr. Bahner was placed in its barren interior and taken to the police station, relieved of the contents of his pockets and his necktie, and placed in a dirty, smelly cell with two unpleasantly drunken persons. Constable Muir at this point discovered that under the facts, Mr. Bahner could not be charged with obtaining goods on false pretences. Instead of releasing him, the policeman went to Mr. Bahner's cell and told him that although he would not be charged with this offence, he would be charged with being intoxicated in a public place.

At trial, the court was convinced that this intimidation was an afterthought on the part of Constable Muir, who realized he had made a grave error, but instead of admitting it and releasing the accused with the appropriate apologies, sought to protect himself by laying a baseless charge not previously mentioned or thought of. Mr. Bahner was removed to another cell and kept there until the next morning when he was released on bail.

Mr. Bahner was subsequently tried in Vancouver City Police Court on Constable Muir's charge of "intoxication in a public place." Muir was the only person who gave evidence, in spite of the fact that a plethora of individuals and restaurant guests were available to give evidence but were not called by the Crown.

The Magistrate hearing the case doubtless formed the same opinion, because he dismissed the charge without even calling for a defence.

The court determined that there were two false imprisonments of Mr. Bahner; the first when Rocky the security guard barred the exit, and the second when Constable Muir, without warrant, took him into custody and jailed him. In all likelihood, the court felt, Constable Muir had in his mind some confused notion that failure to pay for a thing ordered was a crime, but he did not exactly know what crime it was. It was also felt that the attitudes of the manager and the house detective may have influenced Constable Muir's thinking. The court went so far as to say that "the arrogance and stupidity of the conduct of the hotel authorities cannot be over-stated."

Both the hotel and Constable Muir were ordered to pay damages to Mr. Bahner amounting to approximately 759 times the value of the bottle of wine. Mr. Bahner and the Duncans did the dining: guess who did the whining?

It's Three Stooges Time

Notwithstanding the fact that the New York Court of Appeal never once mentioned Curly, Larry and Moe, it is our sincere belief that the Three Stooges planned this whole thing.

Helen Palsgraf stood on a platform owned by the Long Island Railroad Company. She had just bought a ticket to go to Rockaway Beach. A train, bound for a destination of no consequence, pulled into the station and stopped. Two men ran forward to catch it just as it began to leave. One of the men reached the platform of the car and leaped upon it without any mishap. The other man, who was carrying a package, also jumped aboard the car but did not do as well as his companion and appeared to be fairly unsteady, as if he were about to fall. A guard on the car who had held the door open reached forward to grab him in while another guard on the platform rushed forward to push him up from behind. During this whirl of activity, the man's package fell from his arms to the rails. It was a small package and wrapped in newspaper. In fact, although nothing about the package or its appearance would have given anybody any indication of what it contained, it held fireworks.

When the package hit the rails, the fireworks exploded. The shock of the explosion smashed a set of weigh scales twenty-five to thirty feet down the platform and threw them forcefully down. Unfortunately, they landed on poor Mrs. Palsgraf, causing her substantial injury.

Mrs. Palsgraf sued the railroad company. The New York Court of Appeal had quite a difficult time with this situation. In fact, they had such a difficult time that four out of the seven judges gave one decision and three came to a different conclusion. Chief Justice Cardozo gave the majority judgment, pointing out that where no hazard was apparent to the eye of an ordinarily vigilant individual, an act that is innocent and harmless at least to the outward appearance could not be determined to be a tort (coming from the french word for "wrong"). The conduct of the defendant railroad guard was not a wrong in relation to poor Mrs. Palsgraf, standing far away. Nothing in the situation gave notice that the package had in it the potential for peril to persons so far removed. This would not mean, of course, that a party launching a destructive force would be relieved from responsibility for the damage caused, as long as the force was known to the party to be destructive even though they could not foresee the unexpected path that the injury would take.

The court finally concluded that there was nothing in the situation to suggest even to the most cautious person that the parcel wrapped in

newspaper would wreck the station. If the guard had thrown it down knowingly and wilfully, he still would not have threatened the plaintiff's safety, because its appearance would not warn him of its danger. Negligence in the abstract is not a wrong.

Mr. Justice Andrews, reasoning for the minority, came to the opposite conclusion. Not only, he said, would Mrs. Palsgraf not have been injured but for the explosion, the explosion was also the direct cause of her injuries. The fact that she was not blown to the ground by the concussion but by a weighing machine falling upon her as a result of the explosion did not break the sequence. Since injury in some form under the circumstances, was most probable, whether from flying fragments, broken glass, or the wreckage of machines, Mrs. Palsgraf was injured as a result of the negligence of the guards of the railroad.

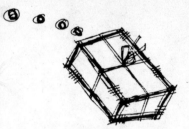

Quite amazing when you think of it. There's poor innocent Helen standing at the far end of a platform, clutching her ticket, minding her own business, and two individuals, almost as innocent, but carrying a concealed and dangerous commodity in a package that was innocuous enter the scene. Had Helen been able to determine the identity of the two individuals, they would certainly have been made a party to this action and the result would have been substantially different. Here, however, the railroad was also treated as an innocent party, as the guards could not possibly have known the contents of the package and were merely acting to assist a passenger whom they perceived to be in potential difficulty. This balancing act between innocent parties happens quite often in our legal system, with the result that both the court and the parties involved feel like extras in the world of the Three Stooges.

Dr. Granato stated that he had removed the male genitalia of Dr. Richards and his external genital appearance was now that of a female. Internally, Dr. Richards's sexual structure is similar to that of a woman who had undergone a total hysterectomy and ovariectomy. Dr. Richards also underwent endocrinological testing and female hormones were administered, giving her the hormonal balance of a woman. All this was accompanied, according to Dr. Granato, with a decrease of muscle mass which meant that Dr. Richards had no unfair advantage when competing against other woman.

The USTA instituted the requirement for *women* to take the Barr Body Test during the 1976 U.S. Open after Dr. Richards applied to play in *women's* singles in the Open. The association indicated that their primary concern in instituting the test was to insure fairness, claiming that there is a competitive advantage for a male who has undergone "sex-change" surgery as a result of his physical training and development while biologically a male. A spokesman for the USTA stated that "there are as many as ten thousand transsexuals in the United States and many more female impersonators or imposters. . . . Because of the millions of dollars of prize money available to competitors . . . the USTA has been especially sensitive to its obligation to assure fairness of competition among athletes. . . . The USTA believes the question at issue transcends the factual background or medical history of an applicant."

Professional tennis players, Françoise Durr, Janet Newberry, and Kristen K. Shaw each stated that, based on her experience, "the taller a player is, the greater advantage a player has . . . similarly, the stronger a player is, the greater advantage the player has, assuming like ability."

Dr. Leo Wollman, who had treated over seventeen hundred transsexual patients, including Dr. Richards, classified the plaintiff as a female. Dr. Richards, he said, has the external genital appearance, internal organ appearance, genital identity, endocrinological makeup, psychological and social development of a female, and in his opinion would be considered as such by any reasonable test of sexuality.

Billie Jean King, holder of hundreds of tennis titles, including Wimbledon and the U.S. Open, and who defeated male tennis professional Bobby Riggs, submitted an affidavit in support of Dr. Richards's application. She and Dr. Richards had been doubles teammates in a tournament, and she had participated in two other tournaments in which Dr. Richards played. In Billie Jean King's judgment, Dr. Richards did not enjoy physical superiority or strength which gave her an advantage over other women competitors in the sport of tennis.

The Rat Race

The brothers Pike had a farm at Beer Seaton, in Devonshire, England. The Bovey Barton Farm, as it was called, was made up of about 425 acres. In addition to a milking parlour there was a dairy, grain store, piggeries, a Dutch barn, and a building referred to as a barley cattle shed where beef cattle were kept in deep litter. Old William Tremiah, he worked on that farm as a herdsman. A good portion of his work was carried on in the milking parlour, but he also spread hay on the fields from time to time, and frequently, farming not being the cleanest occupation, found occasion to wash his hands in the farm water trough.

Now on this farm, there were some rats . . . lots of rats. In fact, the barley cattle shed, grain store, and stacks in the Dutch barn were very attractive to rats. There was what the judge in this case would eventually call a growing population of rats in and around the farm buildings and the farmyard. This farm was running a "rat race" and the rats were winning. It was also determined that a prudent and experienced farmer, once these facts came to his knowledge, would call in the public rodent officer or a contractor to rid the farm of these rodents.

William was not bitten by an infected red-eyed rat, nor did he ingest goods contaminated by these pests. William contracted leptospirosis, also called Weil's Disease, and for this he sued his employers.

Popular scientific knowledge established that leptospirosis was present in 40 to 50 percent of the rats in England. The disease passed from the kidneys to the rats' urine for two to three days if they were in wet or damp conditions. In some cases, Weil's Disease can be fatal. William was fortunate. He did not suffer permanent damage to his liver or kidneys. He did, however, suffer post-infection arthritis, was in hospital for fourteen days, and after that suffered from muscular aches and stiffness. Once he returned to work, his ankles, knees, and fingers swelled, particularly after heavy lifting.

It was impossible to determine exactly where or when William became infected but "on a balance of probabilities" (meaning a 51 percent chance in our legal system), he became infected from the farm.

You could judge that since the Pike brothers knew about the problem, did nothing to prevent it, and William was subjected to infection at the farm, he would have what non-lawyers call an "airtight" case. In fact, there is no disease caused by rats other than leptospirosis which is not associated either with rat bites or food contamination.

Our system is not that simple.

Knowledge of Weil's Disease, in the court's opinion, was as rare as the disease itself. A farmer would be clueless about an explosion of the rat

population, a farmer would take precautions to protect his milk supply, foodstuffs, preserve his animal feed, and generally improve cleanliness, but no more. A farmer would not have in mind the safety of his farm staff in performance of their work as he could not foresee any danger.

You see, in our system, even if someone fails to protect another to whom they have a duty of care, if the damage suffered by the offended party is not *reasonably* foreseeable and/or is too remote, the injured party, in this case William, is out of luck.

The court went on to state: "It would be necessary to introduce protective clothing for the hands and arms, some check on cuts and abrasions, and a system of washing facilities and hygiene, which, in my view, would be out of all proportion in cost and effort to the risk which has to be considered." They added salt to William's wounds; if he had been bitten or had eaten rat-contaminated food, it would have been different.

So let's get this straight: a pair of gloves, long shirt, proper washing facilities, and cut inspection would cost too much and was too much to expect from the Pike brothers. Half the rat population in England is infected and these guys cannot be expected to figure out that would cause someone on the farm to become ill . . .

You know, William, we hear Old MacDonald has a farm. Maybe he treats his herdsmen better!

Police Detain Porky Pigs

The Town of Edwardsville, in Madison County, Illinois, had a serious fellow by the name of Josiah R. Floyd in charge of the local constabulary in 1872. The town was incorporated and had declared many ordinances which Constable Floyd dutifully enforced.

About half a mile outside of Edwardsville lived one Edward L. Friday and his pigs. As fate would have it, one day Friday's porky pigs, squealing with delight, escaped to romp through the Victorian calm of Edwardsville to the utter horror of the local residents.

One of Edwardsville's more serious ordinances proclaimed that the running at large of pigs (or hogs) in the town was a nuisance and therefore prohibited. It went on specifically to direct the police to prevent hogs (or pigs) from running at large, to arrest this behaviour, and place these noisy beasts in the poky under lock and key.

The evidence shows that Friday's pigs were first found running at large by local residents who took it upon themselves to make a citizen's arrest. They believed that a reward of ten cents a head was offered if they could corral these serious miscreants in the local lockup. Poor old Josiah Floyd was not to be written up in the legend books with great law enforcement officers such as Wyatt Earp; the one serious ordinance to be broken in Edwardsville and he was not present to make the bust.

Edward Friday could not secure the release of his pigs from Josiah Floyd's custody. Josiah, who would not bend, had, in fact, a slightly hammish gleam in his eye.

Friday did what any self-respecting pig-owner would do today — he sued. His position was simple. The law gave the police the power to arrest and detain the pigs. Two others had made a citizen's bust. The law, according to Friday, was therefore not followed.

Mr. Justice Sheldon felt hamstrung, but concluded that the two citizens merely helped direct the pigs to the local lockup. Constable Floyd had arrested and incarcerated them, thereby fulfilling all legal requirements.

There was no mention of what Floyd had for dinner on the judgment day . . . one can only speculate.

She Got the Chair – In the Air

Ah, those San Francisco nights: strolling along in the cool air, enjoying the celebratory activities of the citizens on VJ Day when . . . splat! That's right . . . splat. Right out of the sky, a heavy, overstuffed armchair knocked poor Beulah Larson to the ground just after she had stepped out from under the marquee of the St. Francis Hotel.

Although there were numerous people in the immediate vicinity, no one appears to have seen where the flying chair came from or even noticed it until it sat on the sidewalk within a few feet of Ms. Larson's head. Talk about an Excedrin headache. Talk about a definite lack of public perception. Poor Beulah lay unconscious on Post Street, suffering cuts, bruises, abrasions and substantial injuries, and nobody had noticed the assailing armchair.

Beulah sued this once-proud St. Francis Hotel, and her lawyers included as part of her claim a doctrine lawyers call *res ipsa locquitur*. Loosely translated this means "the thing speaks for itself."

For Beulah to win her case, she had to prove:
1. that there was an accident;
2. that the thing that caused the accident was at the time of and prior to the accident under the exclusive control and management of the hotel, and;
3. that the accident would not have happened had the hotel used ordinary care.

The Superior Court of San Francisco found that there was no evidence that the hotel was guilty of any negligence, and the only evidence to connect the hotel to the accident was the fact that the accident occurred in proximity to it. Beulah lost. Beulah was not going to take this lying down. She appealed to the District Court of Appeal of California.

Mr. Justice Bray surmised that the accident was the result of the "effervescence and ebullition of San Franciscans in their exuberance of joy" on VJ Day. He inferred that the chair, though not actually identified as belonging to the hotel, came from some portion of the hotel. Considering the chair's weight, size, the effect of gravity, and the location of the hotel in relation to where the chair came to rest, this was a fairly conservative position to take.

The hurdle for the doctrine to apply remained. A hotel does not have exclusive control of its furniture. Guests have at least partial control. In addition, the accident could still have happened even when the hotel used ordinary care. The mishap would just as likely be due to the fault of a guest or other person as to that of the hotel.

Mr. Justice Bray remained firm in his belief that to keep guests and visitors from launching furniture out of windows would require a guard to be placed in every room in the hotel, and there is no rule of law requiring that of a hotel.

Did you just have the same stomach reaction I did ? Every hotel I have ever stayed in knows how to protect its furniture. In fact, the windows that open are too small to throw out anything but your wallet. Some places do not even provide moveable windows. The lobbies glue down the paintings, screw down the couches, incarcerate the phones. This case took place well in advance of contemporary hotel-management courses.

This all leads us to the sad conclusion that the thing did not speak for itself, or, for that matter, for Beulah; she lost. We hear that she thereafter avoided walking near tall buildings or open windows.

The Besmeared Banker

Andrew Jackson, the seventh president of the United States of America, in discussing a bank renewal bill, called a delegation of bankers he was addressing a den of vipers and thieves and told them he intended to rout them out.

Several years later, American statesman John C. Calhoun referred to the vast surplus of banks as the cohesive power that combined many and various powerful interests greater than the people.

Though the positive image of the pristine banker and the three-piece suit pervades bankers' circles, the public perception is closer to that of President Jackson and his contemporary, statesman Calhoun. Bad loans, both foreign and local, perceived excessive bank charges, and lack of empathy for businessmen and the individual permeates the media and the public perspective.

Michael Brennan, through less-than-fortuitous circumstances, has single-handedly advanced the vision of bankers espoused by America's seventh president in a most peculiar way.

Michael, the President of the Minnesota State Bank, in June of 1989 made use of the bank's executive washroom. Little did he know that while responding to nature's call he would also be subject to its fury.

He went about his business in the usual fashion, but was without warning thrown from his seated position, propelled by two hundred gallons of raw sewage erupting from the bowl beneath him. Michael was forcibly ejected and found himself standing in the cubicle, completely covered in human excrement.

This story was, not unnaturally, seized by the media, giving further humiliation and embarrassment to the already besmeared banker. Michael's attorney sued the Austin P. Keller Construction Co. for damages based on alleged negligence and for the degradation and loss of face he suffered from the story being splashed across Minnesota and the country.

John Brendel, the defendant's attorney, took the position that the explosion of fecal material did not become broadly known until Michael started his lawsuit.

The matter went to trial. The jury foreman sympathized with Michael's experience but stated that they found for the defendant who, in their opinion, acted with a "reasonable" standard of care. The company was not liable even to clean Michael's suit.

Could the members of the jury ever have had the pleasure of applying for a bank loan, a mortgage perhaps? It seems that they could not afford a bank president "routed" out of the bank's executive washroom in one of life's most embarrassing moments more than superficial sympathy.

Michael, we are advised, did not intend to appeal the decision.

FINALÉ

A Bull in a China Shop — *Really*

We have not been playing make-believe. It seems that this expression may really have at its heart a legal source.

This case is not a lot of bull but rather about a bull. Said bull was being driven from a livestock market in Broad Street (it would have had to be), Stamford, England, along a paved public thoroughfare called Ironmonger Street to the premises of Mr. Ward. Pavement and stores lined either side of the street. Mr. Tillett owned a shop on the street, and, after having gone some distance, the bull turned onto the pavement about twelve yards from Mr. Tillett's lovely shop. The beast decided to pass through the open doorway into the shop. Alas, he did not tiptoe through, but virtually ran amok damaging the goods found within.

Mr. Ward's men tried valiantly to drive the animal from the shop and onto the road, but did not meet with much success for about three-quarters of an hour. A bull in a small shop can cause considerable damage in three-quarters of an hour.

The court took pains to point out that this bull, like Ferdinand, was not of "a vicious or unruly nature . . . nor was there anything exceptional in its temper or character." It was just a bull in a china shop through no fault of the defendant, his men (the drovers), nor the bull itself. The law stated where "cattle" go along the highway and there are no fences, this situation is a necessary evil which those whose lands border on the highway must sustain, and the owner of the land must bear the loss.

The court saw no difference in applying this law to a street in a market town or a field in the country. The rule in the court's opinion is very reasonable — get out the crazy glue, Mr. Tillett, and put up a fence.

For this work to end at this point with a lot of bull seems appropriate. As we have seen, it sometimes takes two judges to try a cow, and cases sometimes deal with a lot of bull.

But the kaleidoscope colourfully goes around. Seeking out the legal merry-go-round, the kissing judges, the hustlers, the lucky and not so lucky, the human shields, and serrated guests contributes a fascinating element to the sometimes strange and wacky world of the law.

Acknowledgements

I would like to thank the following people who have contributed to the creation of this book:

- my wife, Fran for her love, support, and honesty;

- my children, Leah, Steven, and Carly, who are my joy and inspiration;

- my brother, Erwin, whose support, input, and opinion are valued more than he knows;

- my parents, Adolph and Faye, who taught me never to surrender my goals;

- my in-laws Max and Gloria Chodak, for all their interest, guidance, and reinforcement;

- my legal assistant and friend, Marilyn Dichter, without whose help and support I would not be where I am today;

- my para-legal, Cindy Applegath, who has had to put up with my insanity on a daily basis to have this book completed;

- my friend, Yaacov Erez, for his help and encouragement;

- my accountants and friends, Ken Finklestein and Alan Desseau, whose opinions and help were always forthcoming;

- my friend, Lou Nigro, who guided me through the publishing process;

- my illustrator David Shaw, editor Sarah Reid, and type designer Robert MacPherson, who all have put forth a great deal of effort and work to achieve a finished product;

- my friend Abe Flohr, who spent countless hours assisting me in researching cases for the book;

- my friend, Laurie-Anne Jones, whose assistance helped bring this project to completion;

- my brother-in-law and sister-in-law, Brian and Gayla Rogers, who are always there for me;

- And most of all my late brother-in-law Eric, my collaborator, my friend. Eric I miss you.

❖ List of Abbreviations

All England Reports	All E.R.
Appeal Cases	A.P.
British Columbia Supreme Court	B.C.S.Ct
Canadian Cases on the Law of Torts	C.C.L.T.
Chancery Division	C.T.
Construction Law Reports	C.L.R.
Criminal Reports	C.R.
Dominion Law Reports	D.L.R.
Federal Reporter	F., F.2d
Federal Supplement	F. Supp.
New Brunswick Reports	N.B.R.
New Zealand Supreme Court	N.Z.S.Ct.
North Eastern Reporter	N.E.
North Western Reporter	N.W.
Ontario Reports	O.R.
Probate Division	P.
Queen's Bench	Q.B.
Reports of Family Law	R.F.L.
Southern Reporter	So.
State Reports Queensland	S.R.Q.
Western Law Times	W.L.T.
Western Weekly Reports	W.W.R.

❖ Source Notes

Page 9; *Law Times*, Feb. 22, 1991. P. 17

Page 11; (1957), 23 W.W.R. 210 (B.C.S.Ct.)

Page 15; *The Lawyer's Weekly*, Mar. 29, 1991. P. 21

Page 16; *Ibid*, Sept. 1, 1989. P. 15

Page 18; (1958) All E.R. 342

Page 21; (1966) S.C.R. 561

Page 25; (1969) 3 All E.R. 1528

Page 27; 127 F. Supp. 730

Page 30; (1956) S.C.R. 991

Page 32; (1971) 2 O.R. 393

Page 35; 84 So. 37

Page 38; (1980) 1 W.L.T. 174

Page 40; Vol. XX Ch. D. 659

Page 45; (1957) 98 C.L.R. 249 (Australia)

Page 47; (1942) 6 L.R. 281 (N.Z.S.Ct.)

Page 51; (1948) A.C. 274 (H.L.)

Page 52; (1984) 55 N.B.R. (2d) 90

Page 54; (1959) O.R. 419 (H.C.J.)

Page 56; (1947) 1 All E.R. 29

Page 57; 9 D.L.R. (3d) 632

Page 59; (1921) 49 O.L.R. 15 (H.C. of J)

Page 61; (1954) 3 All E.R. 59

Page 65; (1975) 20 R.F.L. 112 (Man. Co. Ct.)

Page 67; (1872) 63 Illinois 99

Page 69; (1953) 2 D.L.R. 418 (B.C.S.Ct.)

Page 70; 358 P. (2d) 344

Page 72; (1990) 1 O.R. (3d) 569

Page 75; (1927) S.R.Q. 75

Page 76; 2 C.C.L.T. 218

Page 79; 19 Am. Rep. 350

Page 81; (1872) 63 Illinois 553

Page 83; 52 N.E. (N.Y.) 679

Page 87; 20 N.W., 2d series 28 (Iowa)

Page 89; (1973) W.W.R. 4, 483 (B.C.C.A.)

Page 93; 1980 (1) W.L.T. 85

Page 94; *The Lawyer's Weekly*, May 17, 1991, Vol. II, No. 3

Page 96; *Ibid*, April 19, 1991. P. 3

Page 98; L.A. App. 288 So. 2d, 69; L.A. App. 337 So. 2d, 596

Page 100; (1890) W.L.T. 64

Page 101; 724 F. 2d 831 (1984)

Page 105; (1933) 3 D.L.R. 260

Page 108; 53 D.L.R. (2d) 436

Page 113; (1944) 2 D.L.R. 61

Page 115; 72 O.R. (2d) 417

Page 121; *Law Times*, May 28 – June 3, 1990, p. 1

Page 123; 1 Q.B. 730

Page 125; 75 O.R. (2d) 310

Page 127; (1958) 14 D.L.R. (2d) 333

Page 129; 74 O.R. (2d) 92

Page 131; 66 Penn. St. 411 at p. 377

Page 135; 175 English Reports 764

Page 137; United States *v* Holmes 1842 1 WALL Jr. 1

Page 141; 27 *New York Supplement*, 2d Series, 198

Page 144; 6 D.L.R. (3rd) 322

Page 147; 162 *North Eastern Reporter*, 99

Page 151; *The Lawyer's Weekly*, May 3, 1991, 13 (*see* R. *v* Lucas 1101-13 17 pp.)

Page 152; 400 *New York Supplement*, 2d series 267

Page 155; (1969) 3 All E.R. 1303

Page 159; (1872) 63Ill. 553 at p. 50

Page 160; 188 *Pacific Reporter*, 2d series 513

Page 163 *The Lawyer's Weekly*, August 30, 1991, p. 4

Page 165; (1882) 10 Q.B. 17